Long Run Solution

What I Like Best about Running – and Do Most as a Runner

By Joe Henderson

Cover photo from Boston Marathon, 1976.
(by Jeff Johnson)

Joe Henderson was for more than 30 years a columnist and editor at *Runner's World* magazine, and he has published more than 30 books. He's a veteran of more than 700 races, from sprints to ultras. He teaches running classes at the University of Oregon in Eugene and coaches a local marathon team. His columns appear on his website, joehenderson.com.

Long Run Solution was originally published in 1976 by World Publications. All rights returned to the author with that edition went out of print. This book, reissued in 2010, and other books by the author are now available in three different formats: (1) in print from Amazon.com; (2) as e-books from Amazon.com and BarnesandNoble.com; (3) as printable and shareable PDFs from Lulu.com. The titles:

Home Runs: Moving on and settling down in the post-peak years.

Joe's Journal: Running, as Marathon & Beyond *columnist Joe Henderson sees, practices and teaches it.*

Long Run Solution: What I like best about running, and do most as a runner.

Long Slow Distance: The humane way to train.

Marathon Training: Proven 100-day programs for successful finishes.

Run Right Now: What a half-century of running has taught. (Not available as an e-book.)

Run Right Now Training Log: Set goals, record your progress, and take your running to the next level.

Starting Lines: Early efforts of a writing runner, and where they led.

Coming soon:

Going Far: Reflecting on the years when running grew up, and a writing career took off.

About the author:

Slow Joe: Joe Henderson and his LSD (long slow distance) writings that changed running, by Rich Englehart. (Available only as an e-book.)

Contents

Foreword

by Rich Benyo

(editor, Marathon & Beyond *magazine, which serialized this book in 2003 and 2004)*

Pioneers in various fields often miss the sweet smell of success that they well deserve because their timing is just a bit off or they are at the wrong place at the right time. They are just a mite ahead of their time and thereby miss the fame and fortune bestowed upon those blessed with good timing and sterling placement. The two major North American gold rushes are cases in point: James Marshall, who discovered gold in the mill race at Coloma, California, in 1848, as well as the owner of the property on which it was discovered, Johann Sutter, never profited from 'their' gold, and in fact they died destitute.

Two polar opposites, tall, lean, and hawkish Robert Henderson and laid-back well-rounded George Washington Carmack, in a ballet bordering on Greek tragedy, discovered gold in the Klondike in 1896, but neither would reap the huge rewards their discovery precipitated.

It's similar, in some ways, when contemplating the best-seller running book gold rush at the start of the running revolution in the mid-1970s. Several of the pioneers had long been standing knee deep in the frigid waters panning for gold in the stream of long-distance running.

Hal Higdon, who did not toil exclusively in running but who worked several streams (auto racing, true crime), wrote a landmark book in 1971 (Henry Regnery Company, Chicago) titled *On the Run From Dogs and People*. It is still in print today and deserves to stay in print forever, but it is revered by only a few.

Joe Henderson, who became the editor of Runner's World in 1970 after a stint at *Track & Field News* and who lured Dr. George Sheehan into the pages of *Runner's World* after their meeting on a 1968 Olympic Games tour, had written numerous running books: *Long Slow Distance: The Humane Way to Train* (1969), Run Gently, Run Long (1974) and *Long Run Solution* (1976). As an editor he had shepherded a mass of George Sheehan's *RW* columns into *Dr. Sheehan on Running* (1975). That's a lot of placer mining without hitting the mother lode.

But the whole landscape was to change, and all within the space of a year. Bantam Books bought *Dr. Sheehan on Running* and in 1976 published it as a mass-market paperback — and it took off. In 1977 reformed fatty smoker Jim Fixx, who had been saved by running and who had spent a year mining the ore pockets of long-distance running, including time at the *Runner's World* offices, published his *Complete Book of Running*, which immediately shot to the top of the best-seller lists and stayed there for nearly a year.

George Sheehan would follow up with *Running & Being*, which became a best-seller and a classic. But in all the excitement, *Long Run Solution*, one of the best running books of its generation, was overshadowed, overwhelmed and overlooked.

A handful of rickety-in-the-joints codgers at once lament the book's having been overshadowed by brighter lights while jealously hoarding the memories of the book's flashes of gold and maybe even verging on wanting it to keep its place as 'our' favorite book of the running revolution.

Joe Henderson's *Long Run Solution* was published in trade paperback for $3.95 by World Publications, the book arm of *Runner's World*. It is not a complicated book and it has no long James Joyce-like run-on sentences, even though it is about running on... and on and on. Joe Henderson doesn't write complicated sentences. He writes spare, insightful sentences, and he strings them together like a stonemason working with emeralds and rubies and sapphires to build not a forbidding edifice but a wall over which he entices us to jump in an effort to get to the other side, where he has been running and playing and extending the joys of childhood well into middle age — and beyond.

"Goals are ends. Destinations. Stopping places. Two things happen with them: either you reach them or you don't. And either way you stop, from satisfaction or from frustration." Pretty simple and pretty profound at the same time.

Joe's little book isn't filled with training advice. It doesn't meet the no-pain-no-gain philosophies. It quotes practical scientists looking at running rather than philosophers who weren't really talking about running when they uttered their profundities.

Joe's book is the simple manifesto of citizen long-distance running at that very critical time. It says, simply, that even if you have graduated from college you can still run — and you don't have to run hard in organized competition until you puke. You can enrich your life (both physically and psychologically) by running gently for an hour a day, occasionally testing yourself against yourself by racing.

But, hey, if you don't feel like running races, that's okay too. Just run for an hour to fulfill your design as a human being, where your largest bones and muscles are in your legs, and for good reason. Lower your pulse rate. Knock your cholesterol down a few notches. Keep your weight down. Feel better. Get addicted to euphoria that is self-generated by becoming the joyful animal you can be.

Joe's message is simple: just do it. His approach was simple: simple sentences, simple running habits.

Certainly, some of the book's references are getting a bit long in the tooth after nearly three decades. And a few references (like Tom Bassler's claim that if you run a marathon you are automatically vaccinated against heart disease; consider Jim Fixx) have proven to be less than scientifically sound. But the book's strengths are its incredible readability and its stone-wall solid approach to making running a part of your life.

There isn't a five-year period in which I don't pick up *Long Run Solution* and read it again, both to bring back the energizing effect of validating long-distance running as an adult pursuit and as an antidote to a too-pressured, too-stressed life.

Over the years I've done what little I could to persuade some publisher somewhere to commission Joe to do an updated edition of *Long Run Solution*. But then I come to my senses and relent. Would I want someone to paint tattoos and nose rings on American Gothic? Or perhaps more appropriate, would I want to see all the characters in a Norman Rockwell painting exhibiting shaved heads?

As with many timeless treasures, *Long Run Solution* has the power to circle around through decades of time to take another pass over the stadium, and in many ways the time is right yet again. Today's long-distance runner enjoying this simple little sport and lifestyle can learn much from this simple little book. Allow it to simplify your life while highlighting it with a golden hue.

New Introduction

(for current edition)

Long Run Solution, my 1976 book, was a sprinter. Title aside, it started fast and finished early. The book sold well its first two years, as all running books did in the Jim Fixx-inspired sales boom of the late 1970s. Then it stopped selling, as all running books did in the Fixx-inspired glut of the early '80s.

Today hardly anyone remembers *LRS*, now long out of print. One exception is Rich Benyo. He recalls *Long Run Solution* from his early days as editor (and my successor) at Runner's World. Now the editor of *Marathon & Beyond*, he asked in 2003 if the magazine could reprint the book in four installments. He called it "your best."

That might be too strong a word. In topic and tone, none of mine matches *Did I Win?*, the tribute to and biography of George Sheehan. But that really was George's story, which I transcribed for him as he looked over my shoulder from his next life. Of the books that tell what I myself know and love about running, *LRS* is my favorite for these reasons:

1. *LRS* was my first real book. The earlier four were all booklets, none longer than 96 pages. They were training for the book that runs at least twice the length of any before it — which gave it that much more depth.

2. The book is my clearest statement of how I feel about running. Much of what I've written since is touched on here, and most of these feelings have changed little in the meantime.

Long Run Solution wasn't perfect, or even as good as I like to remember it. Before agreeing to its *Marathon & Beyond* revival, I reread the book for the first time in years. Some of the wording is embarrassingly rough or laughably outdated. The book needed another editor, but at the time I edited my own books. That's like a doctor trying to perform surgery on himself.

In the style of a generation ago, the only singular pronouns used were masculine: he, him, his. That doesn't work anymore when nearly 50 percent of runners — and readers — are women. I bragged of my then-nearly 20 years of running. Now every other runner I know has continued as least that long. I portrayed myself as a grizzled veteran at 33. Now I have children older than that. I talked of seven-minute mile training pace as "easy." Now I'd strain to race a single mile that fast.

But the book also talked of reserving an hour a day for ourselves, for the pursuit of happiness as well as health. This I still preach, and practice.

Another reason *Long Run Solution* became my favorite book was its timing. My PRs had hardened into concrete by then, and I'd recently survived my big injury scare (and resulting surgery). The time had come to decide what to do the rest of my running life.

Naming *LRS* as favorite book might sound like a knock on the 15 or so books that followed, but it really isn't. They served purposes, just as races do after the last PR is set.

There is value — even a certain nobility — in keeping going after we've peaked. Which is the message of the book: Do what it takes to run long, not in miles but in years and decades.

Original Introduction

(published in 1976)

California sees runners all the time. There are so many on its streets now that it ignores them. I'd gotten used to being ignored. Then two summers ago I went home to Iowa, to a town so small that a thousand towns its size would fit into San Francisco.

The little town had never seen a runner on its streets and country roads before I started running there in the late 1950s. No one had done it since I left there in the early 1960s.

I'd come full circle. I was thought to be weird when I started running there, then for a while had been the object of some admiration for winning some races, and now I was weird again.

Before, I could pretend I was training to win races and make people there believe it — sometimes even make myself believe it. But now I wasn't a kid working out fantasies any more. I was a man in his 30s with a wife and a child and a job. People in this Iowa town had never seen a grown man run, and couldn't see any sense in one doing it...

I'm running. I've tried my best to avoid people. But here's a man in bib overalls blocking the way.

"Hi there, Fred. Uh, remember me?"

He looks through squinted eyes until a spark of recognition ignites.

"Yeah, I do. You're the Henderson boy. How could I forget? Never seen anyone else running around the way you did. Still doing that, huh?"

"Oh, sure. I guess I've been at it too long now to stop. It's a habit."

"Well," Fred says, "I never seen much sense in that stuff myself. I mean, around and around, and never getting nowhere. What's it get a fella? Seems like a big waste of time to me."

"Maybe so. But if I didn't run, I guess I'd probably weigh 200 pounds."

He chuckles. "Yeah, guess that's something all right. It's hurting nobody, anyway. But you sure do look awful skinny. You need to get some meat on your bones, boy."

Shrug.

"What kind of work you doing now, anyway?"

I answer, "Working for a magazine. A magazine about running."

"Figures."

I edge away and say, "I've gotta run..."

Conversation after conversation went the same way, with the refrain always being "Still running?" Running was what people there remembered me by. And I guess I should be happy to be remembered at all. But the way they asked it seemed to say, "What's a man your age doing still playing around with something as foolish as this?" It was as if I were still playing cowboys and Indians.

People in this town and hundreds of small farming towns like it take a narrow view of what work and play should be, and mine didn't fit.

An honest day's work to them means planting the south 40 with corn, or putting the hay in the barn. It means sweating and getting your hands dirty.

After a working day, the limit of play might be a quick softball game or a little bowling. More likely, the end of the day means a shower and a big meal, the newspaper and a couple of hours of TV, and to bed early.

Farming is heavy physical labor. Running is the same thing. A person who sweats all day on the job doesn't feel much like sweating some more at play — and doesn't have much need to do it.

Running has never gained many converts from people who work with their hands. Runners are mostly people who work with their heads. Running is an essential physical balance to an otherwise mental day.

Nothing works the body while loosening up the mind like a good, honest sweat. If we don't find it in our work, we need it in our play.

Kim Norton, a California college student, surveyed 125 distance runners. His results confirmed what we runners already know. We run mainly to exorcise personal demons, physical and emotional.

Norton's runners said they viewed running first as "a means to health and fitness," and second as a "catharsis" — a way to relieve tension and frustration. Apparently they were getting what they wanted, because they'd been averaging an hour of running a day for several years.

It feels good to run. Well, maybe the run itself isn't always pleasant, but the effects of it usually are. Every runner is so sure of this he wonders why it's so hard to convince people outside of running that this physical and mental glow is real and important.

Dr. Thomas Bassler of Los Angeles has evidence to show that marathon-type training — in units of six miles and more — gives absolute protection against fatal heart disease. Independently, Dr. Ernst van Aaken of Germany has reached a similar conclusion in metric terms — 10,000 meters a day as a minimum for everyone.

Runners and some doctors have suspected this long-term physical benefit for quite a while now. The psychological benefit hasn't gotten so much attention, yet it is even more immediate, dramatic and promising.

San Diego psychiatrist Dr. Thaddeus Kostrubala employs running in his treatment and reports, "I've never experienced this kind of success in psychotherapy before." The successes include a heroin addict kicking his habit and a paranoid schizophrenic returning to school and maintaining a "B" average.

Dr. Kostrubala says distance running produces an "altered state of consciousness that can be called a kind of Western meditation." His parents run for an hour, then go directly to group therapy sessions. It's common, he notes, for them to feel uncomfortable and depressed in the first 20 minutes of their runs. After that, they experience "mild euphoria."

Dr. William Glasser, author of the best-seller *Reality Therapy*, says, "I am certain there is a good physical effect from regular exercise. But I am even more certain that for those who get into running, and do it on a regular basis, something builds which is akin to addiction. That is, if the runner doesn't run, he feels nervous, upset, anxious, tense — a tension which is relieved only by running his prescribed amount of time."

Dr. Glasser quickly adds that this is a positive addiction, built through runs of about an hour. The benefits,

15

he says, are "increased self-confidence and even increased ability to use one's imagination, which of course makes life much more enjoyable."

It's good to know that my 20 years of running might have done more for my heart than any cardiologist could. But it's far better to know that this hour a day may be keeping the psychiatrist away.

1. Explaining

Her eyes were puffy and red around the rims from not being able to fall asleep last night or to wake up this morning. And the cigarette and coffee she was having for breakfast weren't helping much.

The loose-hanging top and baggy pants she wore to hide her 50 extra pounds weren't working either. They looked like canvas thrown over a haystack.

I watched her move through the roomful of patients. Her look mirrored contempt for them. This was an outpatient clinic in the city's ghetto. Most of the patients were black and poor, and tired as well as lame. The big woman was the clinic supervisor. Her job was to take the patients into a tiny side room and read them their rights and responsibilities.

"Henderson!" she shouted, sounding like a drill sergeant.

"Here!" I shouted back, louder than I wanted my voice to be.

"This way," she said, motioning to a door with frosted glass.

She closed the door and ordered, "Sit there." I obeyed without question. There was barely room for both of us inside. She rolled a printed form into a typewriter and snapped out routine questions.

Why was I there? Nothing big. Just needed a routine checkup.

Did I have insurance? No.

Age? Thirty-two.

She raised an eyebrow and said, "C'mon." Then looked closer and decided I wasn't lying. I smiled, smugly satisfied that I still could be mistaken for a younger man, despite the smile lines that betrayed me.

Marital status? Married.

"What does she think of bubbles?" the big woman asked.

"What?" I could make any sense of her question.

"How does your wife stand living with Mr. Bubbles? You're so happy and bouncy, and it's only nine o'clock in the morning. It's enough to make me sick."

I mumbled that sometimes it bothered Janet too. I bother a lot of people that way, to the point that I try to subdue my smile and bounce – particularly the morning. Normal people don't like seeing someone run through their lives with a half-assed grin on his face and a "good morning" bubbling up from the heart, while they are fighting for the energy and will to stay awake.

It's insulting to flaunt health and happiness in front of people who have neither. And they resent it. Everyone talks about being fit and full of joy, but no one does much about it. Anyone who does can expect to be out of step with most of the people around him. Often misunderstood, sometimes ridiculed, occasionally despised.

It's a curious way to spend one's time, running in endless circles pursuing health and happiness. As one who has done it for 20 years now, I'm the first to admit this. I can see why people who don't run this way can't make any sense of it. The logic of it wouldn't stand up to examination by a Philosophy 101 class.

Running traditionally has been a competitive sport. Yet the greatest benefits are said to come from moderate, well-below-all-out effort.

It's just a kid's game which backers claim has the most benefit in curing and preventing grown-up ailments.

This is the simplest way to move, but runners claim it is the catalyst for physical and mental changes so profound that they can't find words to explain them.

The True Believers say they wake themselves up in the morning by tiring themselves out with a run, and that they relax in the evening by working hard.

They assure anyone who'll listen that they've never felt better, while complaining endlessly about their uncooperative legs and their unfulfilled dreams.

The activity which is supposed to fill hearts with new strength and joy has caused more than a few hearts to explode from the unaccustomed stress.

It may sound like I'm coming around to admitting that we runners are hypocrites, or that we feel compelled to explain our madness with rational arguments. But no, I'm not doing either. Every one of those apparent inconsistencies I've just listed has a factual basis. And it takes an entire book to give those facts.

All of the facts are built around one main fact. That is, movement is natural and necessary. Man is made to move on foot, and a certain amount of this movement is essential each day 'to keep body and soul together.

Man survived these thousands of years by chasing down his food or by running away from predators to avoid being eaten. But as he evolved, his brain devised tools that took the work out of food-gathering and self-defense. He reached the point in the past century where his tools were doing all the work. The automobile took over the work of the legs.

"Years ago," wrote Aaron Sussman and Ruth Goode in their book *The Magic of Walking*, "scientists were predicting the evolution of [humans] without legs, thanks to the automobile. Nowadays we know they were wrong. It's not our legs we are losing. It is our minds."

We no longer have to chase down our food or run from our enemies, but we still have to pursue health and happiness. They don't come to us. We have to run after the good feelings and flee the demons.

At 5:30 this morning I felt anything but healthy and happy. The bathroom light came on with a white flash, and my eyes rebelled against opening. When I finally adjusted to the cold light, I looked in the mirror and saw the kind of puffy, red-rimmed eyes that I'd seen on the woman in the clinic.

I tried to stretch the sleep and chronic soreness from my muscles, and they were as pliable as sun-dried leather.

As I stepped out the back door, the darkness and cold tried to throw me back inside.

The first steps were painful and awkward. I slapped and stomped at the pavement, and was aware of each individual footfall – nothing else but one step at a time, and the effort it took and discomfort it radiated.

Five minutes went by. Sweating began. But my form was still ragged.

Ten minutes. The stride smoothed out, but I felt depressed and unwilling to face much more of this.

Then, little by little, as always happens, I forgot about individual steps as they flowed together like raindrops into a stream. Then I forgot all about the vehicle that was carrying me along.

I ran at a pace that let me think about everything except how I was running. My mind wandered and sniffed at subjects like a dog on a morning romp.

The first five minutes seemed like a half-hour. The last half-hour compressed into five minutes. I'd run an hour and felt good almost euphoric. My mind was loose for writing, and I was 150 percent awake. The glow would gradually fade during the day, and tomorrow morning – like every morning – it would have to be renewed. The good of running doesn't store well. The demons always come back.

Sure, I know all about the physical good that supposed to come to people who run: the heart and lungs of a thoroughbred racehorse, the speed of a jungle cat, the endurance of a timber wolf. Runners like to think that they are becoming skinny supermen. And they may be. But this is incidental to me.

I run not for what it might give me tomorrow but for the way it makes me feel today. Running is my carburetor. It regulates and channels energy and enthusiasm, picking me up when I'm down and calming me down when I'm hyper.

Man was born to run, and this is more true for me than most men. If I didn't run, I would weigh 200 pounds instead of 130. I probably would be an insomniac and have an ulcer. I'd be and smoke and/or drink addict.

That's the kind of personality and metabolism I have — compulsive and hyperactive. Without safety valves, I overdo whatever I do — from eating to working. I'm restless, impatient and worrisome. I take on more jobs than I can handle, like a juggler trying to keep 12 eggs in the air at the same time. The compulsion and hyperactivity feed on each other, causing me to accomplish less and less while trying to do more and more.

Running is the safety valve.

No use fighting what I am. That would only compound the problems, leaving me frustrated as well as compulsive and hyperactive. So instead of taking tranquilizers and trying to slow down, I've taken my minuses and run with them. The running harmlessly drains away energy which otherwise would gnaw away at my insides.

I'm never so relaxed as after I've pushed myself. If I sat here and commanded myself, "Relax!" I couldn't do it. By telling my muscles to go slack, just the opposite would happen. But if I double up my fist, make the tightest ball possible and squeeze it until my arm shakes, hold it for many seconds then let go, I'm perfectly relaxed without trying.

The same happens in running. Running is several thousand "body clenches," done one after another, rhythmically. Tighten and relax, tighten and relax, tighten and relax. After the first 10 or 20 minutes, you feel as if a plug has been pulled and the tension is draining out through your toes.

Movement is strong medicine — stronger yet safer than any tranquilizer. But it has to be a certain kind of movement to do its best work.

Forget all about being an athlete. Forget everything you ever knew about training to go fast. The training for speed works against the style of running you want to cultivate, which is training for sanity.

I'm not saying you must always cruise along as cautiously as a little old lady who only drives her car to the store and to church on Sundays, and who never shifts into high gear. Part of sanity training is blowing out the carbon once in a while at red-line pace. But that's only a small part of the whole routine — not the only reason for running as it is with athletes.

Athletes are taught three Golden Rules:

1. *Aim for the stars.*
2. *Work hard to get there.*
3. *Sidestep anything which gets in your way.*

High goals, hard work and sacrifice take athletes where they want to go in a hurry... Or if they don't get there, they are in and out of the sport in a hurry. The emphasis in athletics is on speed, and athletes are impatient to reach top speed in a hurry.

For running to keep yielding sanity, though, it has to last. The good effects aren't stored. They have to be freshened almost every day. For anyone to run every day, he must (1) stay healthy, (2) stay fresh and (3) stay eager. In other words, don't get broken down, run-down or bored.

The way to do that is to run with precisely the opposite Golden Rules from those of athletes:

1. *Aim low.*
2. *Work easily.*
3. *Sacrifice nothing.*

Goals may be essential for athletes who aren't looking farther ahead than the end of the season. But they aren't much help to someone who wants to stay healthy and happy.

Goals are ends. Destinations. Stopping places. Two things happen with them: either you reach them or you don't. And either way you stop, from satisfaction or from frustration.

Most runners adopt the goals of the few who climb highest — meaning most of us are frustrated because we're always scrambling toward peaks which are never reached. The minute we see what's happening, the minute we look up and see we're no closer to the top than when we started the ascent, we're through. Very few runners slip back down gracefully.

I prefer a flatter, more circular kind of running. The idea is not to scale peaks no one has even climbed before, to go up once and then stop, but to keep circling the flat little loops which anyone could run.

In the last week, I've probably run 40 miles, maybe 50. I'm not sure, because I'm not counting. In the last year this might add up to 2000 miles — in the 20 years I've been running, 30,000 or 40,000 miles. But again I have no way of knowing.

I don't want to know, because if I kept track of my running this way, I'd be poorer for it. I'd start to feel like a pocket calculator. Numbers would be more important to me than experiences. Worse, I'd always have more mountains to climb. I would look up every morning and see a peak I thought I had to reach, a quota I had to meet.

Such hulking obstacles would scare me. But there's nothing at all imposing or frightening about a few miles each day. So I never look any further ahead than tomorrow or much further back than yesterday. I divide the runs up into easily handled chunks and take care of them one at a time, because seven days times seven miles doesn't sound nearly as far as 49 miles a week.

If you take care of the days, the weeks and months take care of themselves.

The first step in making running easy is to take it in small, appetizing bites which go down pleasantly. The second step is to fall into a comfortable pace.

I mean "long" in two senses of the word. One refers to individual runs. For reasons I'll get to later, 30 minutes seems to be a minimum running time. If you want a quick physical jolt, you can get it in less than half that time. But there's a lot more to my running than racing the heart for a few minutes. The mellowness usually doesn't come until later in a long run.

So go slowly enough to keep moving comfortably for the full half-hour and still look forward to more. At first this may mean doing more walking than running. Even as you advance, you may not go much faster than a walk. It doesn't matter. No one's keeping score.

Pace yourself for the length of the run. Don't blow everything in the first mile. This concept is easy to understand. But it's a little harder to grasp the idea of longer-term pacing and to use it — how to pace yourself over *years* as well as half-hour and hours.

If you're like me, you're a "lifer." Your career stretches out ahead of you like a marathon, so one day is like a few inches, a year is a few hundred yards. Keep in mind when you're tempted to rip through a year or two at top speed what this might mean to the pace later on.

Long-term running is a habit developed through years of repetition. It's a normal and natural part of each day — *a part* of, not *apart* from, everyday living. It doesn't dominate the day but occupies a special place in it. The daily run is a plus, not a minus. It adds to the quality of the day, never subtracts from it.

Yet most exercise writers and running coaches introduce this activity by telling what you have to give up to be a runner. They talk of "can'ts" and "don'ts." They say, in effect, "The harder it is, the worse it feels, the better it is for you."

I want none of that. Running can be most positive. In fact, I'd go so far as to say if you want to keep at it, it has to be positive. You have to think of what it gives you, not what you're giving up. Think not in terms of "can'ts" and "don'ts" but of the things you can do only because you run.

Make running not something you *have* to do, but something you *want* to do — something you do almost unconsciously from day to day but miss terribly when it isn't there one day.

I say, "aim low," but that's not the same as running aimlessly. Everyone needs a direction, a purpose. I have one driving ambition, but it isn't like most goals. I aim to keep going rather than looking for stopping places.

"Run easily," I say. But that means running easily most of the time. Occasionally, everyone needs to go hard — not to win races but to satisfy a need to test oneself, to take chances.

"Make running a regular and normal part of the day," I say. But at the same time, set it apart as a special, almost sacred time. Stake out at least an hour a day for yourself and let nothing or no one intrude on it.

It doesn't have to be a full hour of running. Some of it can be walking. But it should be an hour where you get primitive again. Ride no machines. Read no books or magazines or newspapers. Listen to no radios or phonographs. Watch no TV. Write on no pages.

Run alone for undisturbed thinking. Run with a few friends for uncluttered conversations. Run to slow down, and to exercise a body and brain which don't get much chance to work without mechanical crutches.

I run gently — not always gently but only adding enough hard work to make me appreciate the easy. I run an hour a day — not an hour every day but as an average. I run because it's fun and it feels good — not always equally fun and good but that way in its total effect. In a week's time, one run leaves me euphoric, two produce a mild glow, in three more I'm going through the motions, and one day I should have stayed in bed. All the days are important, since the good ones come as surprises and are sweetened by the bad.

The contrasts are reasons to run, Amby Burfoot once wrote. And he's proof that a sensible, relaxed attitude and race-winning ability can co-exist, since he won the 1968 Boston Marathon.

Amby said, "I run because I enjoy it — not always, but most of the time. I run because I have always run — not trained, but run. What do I get? Joy and pain. Good health and injuries. Exhilaration and despair. A feeling of accomplishment and a feeling of waste. The sunrise and the sunset."

I can't remember how many times I've borrowed those words when my own have failed me. Or those of George Sheehan, running's thinker laureate, when I'm asked to tell why I approach running as I do.

Dr. Sheehan wrote, "For every runner who tours the world running marathons, there are thousands who run to hear the leaves and listen to the rai, and look to the day when it is suddenly as easy as a bird in flight. For them sport is not a test but a therapy, not a trial but a reward, not a question but an answer."

I've never been rich or fast enough to tour the world. But I have been around the country, chasing fast miles and later marathons. I thought catching up with them would give me happiness. I caught most of the times I wanted, but no sooner did I touch them than they spirited away again. I wanted more and chased harder, and grew frustrated and eroded my health.

Only in the last few years have I come to know that health and happiness aren't found at the end of a long, hard pursuit but during a gentle, never-ending pursuit itself.

Running this way wins you no races or admirers. You impress no one by running gently and running long, because you go against the grains of both the serious runners and the confirmed non-movers.

Your energy and enthusiasm mock people who don't have them. It's an implied insult to the way they live and work — both to those who don't do anything physical and think you do too much, and to those who attack their activity with single-minded fury and think you are wishy-washy.

Serious runners will sneer as they call you "Fun-Runner" or "Jogger." Non-runners will call you names like "Mr. Bubbles," and wonder what the hell you're high on when you have a bouncy step and wear a smile at nine in the morning.

You have to be satisfied with impressing yourself a little bit, knowing you're holding on by a thread to fitness and sanity which something or someone is conspiring to take away at every turn.

2. Addicting

"Why would anyone want to do something which is at best boring and at worst painful?"

I've been asked that enough times over the last 20 years, in enough different ways, and have gotten enough uncomprehending stares at my answers that I've all but quit answering people who don't have the experience to understand.

The assumption is that runners are dull-witted, like the ponies which plod around in circles all day long at carnival rides, and that we can think of no more imaginative way to pass our time. The suspicion is that we have masochistic tendencies; that we beat ourselves up for an hour each day because it feels so good to stop.

I know running is boring and painful only at the start, then later on only when a runner goes about it the wrong way. But when trying to tell this to anyone whose experience is the sum of gym-class punishment laps and long Army slogs under full equipment, an abstract platitude like "I enjoy it" won't do.

"Enjoy running?" he'll say. "If you can get turned on by that stuff, you should have your head examined."

So instead of wasting time talking to people who won't listen, I just shrug and say, "I guess I've been doing it so long I don't know how to stop." Then I change the subject.

The non-runner accepts the runner's habit as one he can't break, and one that — while strange and impossible

29

to comprehend — apparently is rather harmless. The habit is less sporting than playing the horses but also less dangerous than heroin addiction.

I don't casually toss out this analogy of running with addiction. There's much more to it than the uninitiated can ever know, and even more than many runners themselves may realize.

Running is habit-forming. It's addictive if done in a certain way for a long enough time. And far from being a destructive habit like tobacco and alcohol can be, the running addiction is a positive one. It may be the central reason why people run long distances and why running agrees with us.

Runners may start because they fear heart disease or loathe the way they look — or because they have visions of awards and records dancing in their heads. But almost everyone grows thin and strong-hearted rather quickly with running. What's the next motivation after he has lost his fear and loathing? And almost no one grows up to be a champion. What's to keep a runner going after he has lost his illusions?

Addiction. Addiction follows a convenient natural timetable which hooks the new runner at about the same time the earlier drives are fading. Being addicted doesn't mean he has given up his interest in being fit inside and out, or that he no longer cares to race. It means he's probably fitter and faster than ever before as a by-product of the addiction.

In other words, like all addicts he has withdrawal symptoms if he misses a day. The usual ones are irritability, sleepy-sluggishness and a vague sense of guilt. These obviously are unpleasant. So to avoid them, the running addict runs every day. Regularity is the key to good training, so he gets better at running. As he gets better, he runs more. The more he runs, the more addicted he becomes. And so on.

Runners now are having their heads examined, as their concerned families and cynical friends have suggested for so long. And the reports from the head doctors say that running does have dramatic psychological effects — almost all of them good ones.

Several reputable psychiatrists are testing running and therapy both for serious mental illnesses and for the neuroses which are so common we think of them as normal. Independently, these doctors are reaching a similar conclusion. Running leads in the general direction of sanity, and runners only stray from that path when they can't run.

There'll be more in later chapters about how running can help straighten out bad head trips. But the subject now is addiction. Establishing it is the first priority of anyone who wants to run for its therapeutic values.

I'd suspected for a long time that something like addiction had taken hold of me after the first year or two of running. The first year, I ran only for the races. When the season ran out, I was relieved to be done with it until the next spring. The following winter, I noticed I was back where I'd started in terms of condition. So I began training early for the season. I read somewhere, "If you hope to get anywhere in this sport, you must train year-round." I kept running after the second season — still more for the racing than any attachment to running itself.

Then in the third year, I realized I was hooked when the winter temperature sunk to 29 below zero and snow piled up so high I almost could walk out my second-floor bedroom window onto it. I found I was leaving my bicycle at home on these mornings, not because the streets were too slick for riding my paper route but because I preferred to run it — in the cold, in the dark, at 5:30 a.m. That's addiction, though it was 10 years later before I heard anyone call it by that name.

The first I read of it was in the early 1970s. A doctor named Frederick Baekeland was trying to test the results of "exercise deprivation" among habitually active people. The doctor offered to pay them to take a month off.

The reaction of the addicted exercisers was possibly more significant than anything Baekeland found in his formal study: "Many prospective subjects — especially those who exercised daily — asserted that they would not stop exercising for any amount of money."

Baekeland had to take people who exercised only every other day. And during their month of inactivity, even they showed the classic symptoms of withdrawal: irritability, anxiety, tension, frustration, guilt.

What I've said so far seems to suggest that runners are running to escape — that we are running away from the pain of not running and from the demons in ourselves.

True, but only partly true. If this were the only reason to run, running would be little different from the negative addictions which lead away from something bad and toward something worse. Running leads from a negative to a positive.

It's a time when the medical advice is running to extremes. On the one hand, Dr. Meyer Friedman and Dr. Ray Rosenman write in *Type A Behavior and the Heart* that running is a form of "mass suicide" which is destroying hearts instead of saving them. Dr. J.E. Schmidt writes a sensationalized article for *Playboy* which tells how running tears apart the back and legs. Dr. Peter Steincrohn writes in his syndicated column that it is a disgusting post-adolescent fad which will soon fade away. These are non-runners offering other non-runners ready-made excuses for continuing what they're not doing.

At the other extreme are Dr. Thomas Bassler and several of his associates in the American Medical Joggers Association, Dr. Ernst van Aaken in Germany and, admittedly, myself. (I of course have no medical standing, but act as a parrot for a special point of view.) We say regular long and slow runs — an hour or six miles — are needed to stay healthy. We are runners offering justification to those who already are doing what we say.

There is little understanding between the two extremes because neither is willing to admit that the other might have a point. The anti-running doctors exaggerate to make their point — yet it is a fact that runners do have an occasional heart attack, do have frequent injuries and do take it up and drop it quickly because it is a fad. The pro-running people have a point that an hour a day keeps the doctor away. But I think they emphasize the wrong kinds of doctors. It may not be the cardiologists and orthopedists and podiatrists so much as the psychologists and psychiatrists.

Both extremes must realize that we long-term runners keep going even if there is no promise of a physical Nirvana, even if there are some risks, because we are hooked on the physical high which running a half-hour or more each day can produce.

The first person to describe this phenomenon rationally and objectively was Dr. William Glasser, a Los Angeles psychiatrist who is best known for his book *Reality*

Therapy. Dr. Glasser is not a distance runner, so perhaps his impressions mean more than those of one of us. He has no vested interest, no reason to show running in its best possible light.

Glasser has formalized the concept of "positive addiction" [PA] in a book by that title. In it, he says running is "the hardest but surest way" to reach this healthy state.

"Positive addiction," he writes, "increases your mental strength and is the opposite of negative addiction, which seems to sap the strength from every part of your life except the area of the addiction... The positive addict enjoys his addiction, but it does not dominate his life. Unlike the negative addict who is satisfied completely to live for his addiction, to the exclusion of everything else, a positive addict uses his extra strength to gain more love and more worth, more pleasure, more meaning, more zest from life in general."

This is one of Dr. Glasser's PA principles: that a rather small "fix" goes a long way. He says it is "not something you do all day long. It is not like searching for heroin or drinking alcohol or gambling which may occupy you practically all the time. It is something you do for a reasonable time — usually about an hour a day."

The hour-a-day theme is one which comes up again and again in the advice this book has for runners. I don't think it takes that much time to become hooked. A half-hour may be enough, and if a runner habitually does several hours a day the addiction threatens to become negative by taking too much of his time and energy from other things. But for now, this is Dr. Glasser's platform. Let's hear him out.

"More and more as I study positive addiction in its various forms, it seems that about an hour a day does it.

34

Therefore, if the person who is looking to be positively addicted isn't willing to put in this 40 minutes to an hour a day, there is a good chance that whatever he chooses to become addicted to won't be successful."

When he was first developing his PA theories, Dr. Glasser passed out questionnaires to people in the audiences at his speeches. He was most impressed by the number of runners ("of whom I was at best dimly aware") responding that they were addicted.

He had watched runners stream past his office on San Vicente Boulevard in West Los Angeles and had wondered as non-runners do, "What in the world makes these people run? I didn't think it was possible to do something that seemed to be such a painful drag in order to get some indefinite future payoff like not having a heart attack 20 years later. Even the present payoff of being trim and strong didn't seem that motivating to me."

Glasser then asked to insert a list of questions into *Runner's World* magazine to find what drives these men and women. He expected a trickle of response but heard from more than 700 runners. Something on the order of 80 percent were "positively addicted" by the doctor's definition of the term.

This information led him to write, "I believe that running creates the optimal condition for PA because it is our most ancient and still most effective survival mechanism. We are descended from those who ran to stay alive, and this need to run is programmed genetically into our brains."

It is because we are set up this way, he says, that running takes little conscious control. "When we run without fatigue, we are able to free most of the brain for other activity. When this happens, it is easy to slip into the euphoric, unique PA state."

Since addiction is such an important driving force of runners, a first priority for beginners should be to form as strong a habit as possible, as quickly as possible.

Dr. Glasser already has hinted at how to do this: (1) run for an hour or the better part of it; (2) run at a non-exhausting pace; (3) free the mind to wander.

He adds that one must start with the idea that PA is worth running after, and that it will take a while to catch it. ("It rarely occurs in less than six months no matter what the activity, and some runners say it took them two years... One has to keep going a long time on faith, and most people don't have that much faith.")

Glasser thinks that most of the running should be done alone because the initiative must be one's own (not using a group as a crutch to make up for a personal weakness of will) and "because the PA state is a state of oneness, not a group experience."

Finally, he says that the bulk of the running should be "non-competitive" and "non-self-critical." (In other words, "not only must we not compete with others, we must learn not to compete with ourselves if we wish to reach the PA... I believe that for anyone to go 'out of his mind,' to let his brain spin free in whatever activity he is in, he must learn to engage in the activity in a non-self-critical way.")

This formula, as I'll explain in later chapters, doesn't completely exclude social and speed running. But it puts the emphasis on gentle, solo runs because they are the most direct route to addiction.

Dr. Glasser writes, "To become addicted, you have to reach a PA state on a regular basis — at least several times a week for several minutes to an hour each time. If this happens, then you experience a surge of pleasure which you learn to crave."

This craving keeps you running, and opens the way to everything else running has to offer.

3. Starting

I've run almost every day for 20 years. But this hasn't taught me how to talk with people taking their first steps. You see, I've forgotten what my first ones were like. And even if I remembered, they wouldn't be much help because I was 14 then, and 14-year-olds don't have to go through the same beginning pains as adults do.

Also, my background is in competitive running — and you aren't training to become a competitor. Not yet, anyway. You might want that later, but forget it now. In most ways, training for racing works against the kind of basic fitness you're trying to establish.

My running is fun. Not ha-ha fun, but a quieter kind of contented fun. Not fun every minute of every day, but fun in the overall effect. My running is easy and comfortable, and it feels good. Seldom is there a morning when I don't feel 100 percent better in the last mile of a run than I had in the first mile.

Never is there a day when I don't look forward to my run. Sometimes I don't want to go very far or fast, but I always want to go.

Never is my running boring, because never are two runs exactly the same. They may be the same distance, at the same pace, over the same course at the same time of day. But they're subtly different. You learn to appreciate the subtleties.

But the first weeks, maybe even months, of running will be no fun. It will be tiring. It will hurt. Even the slowest shuffle will be difficult because you're asking your body to do something it hasn't done in a long time — if ever. You will dread it because no sane person looks forward to pain. It will bore you because you aren't yet experiencing anything except your fatigue, and boredom and fatigue are close relatives.

All I can do is ask you to bear up. Be strong and patient. Promise yourself you'll stick out this break-in period, and I promise you much better days to come.

While it's true I haven't ever been a true beginner, I've watched hundreds of people begin — and only a small minority of those survived long enough to enjoy running and taste its benefits.

People drop out for one main reason: they treat exercise as a vile-tasting prescription drug to be forced down quickly. They allow five or 10 or 15 minutes for a run, hold a stopwatch in their sweaty fists, and race the prescribed distance as fast as their flabby legs and lungs and hearts will carry them. They have to do the distance faster today than yesterday, faster tomorrow than today. It escalates until they hit a wall.

Dr. Meyer Friedman, in his best-seller *Type A Behavior and the Heart*, violently objects to running as an exercise because he says it creates a sense of urgency. The only kind of running he knows is the rushed kind I've described. He sees the results in patients whose hearts have given out from the pace.

I see the results in running dropouts whose legs break down and whose minds are blown by the strain of chronic racing. So I'm Dr. Friedman's unlikely ally in opposing this kind of running.

To start running, get hurt or discouraged and quit after a few days or weeks is worse than never having started—because now you're not only in as bad shape as ever, but you are convinced that the cure is worse than the ailment.

Right from the start, I want you to take an easier, safer, more positive and more lasting course — one even Dr. Friedman may approve of if he knew it existed.

Start with a few simple guidelines (a word I prefer to "rules"):

1. *Make exercise an everyday habit* — an essential part of each and every day, something you look forward to and miss if it isn't there.

2. *Set aside a full hour each day for yourself and your activity.*

3. *Pace yourself for the long haul* — "long" in terms of individual runs but even more so in terms of years. Start with the idea that you're going into this for life.

I can sum up these three points by saying, "Don't rush it too much or push it too hard." A habit can't take root in a mind that is always harried or a body that is always hurting.

Running has attracted a lot of attention — not all of it good — from doctors. Several years ago, they were pretty much in favor of it. Now, as they see its damage, they aren't so sure.

Even the severest critics — Dr. Friedman is their leader — admit there are some benefits on the physical side: weight loss, muscle toning, heart-lung strengthening.

But even the staunchest friends of running are slow in recognizing and promoting its psychological effects —

which are more immediate and profound than anything that happens physically.

Psychiatrists only now are seeing what longtime distance runners have always known — that running acts as an addictive drug which bends the mind in nice ways.

The kind of running-jogging recommended in most texts for beginners — 10-15 minutes every other day is a common prescription — is enough to give a quick, violent workout but probably not enough to form a lasting habit.

Those first 10-20 minutes are rather distasteful preliminaries — for everyone, seasoned runners as well as beginners. This is a warmup. It takes this long to convince yourself that you're serious about working and that the body should cooperate. There's always this early struggle.

I know a woman runner who jogged a token 10-15 minutes a day for more than a year. "To tell you the truth," she said, "I despised it. I said to myself, 'What a horrible way to exercise this is.' I did it more from a sense of duty than anything else, mainly to please my husband who is a marathoner. I couldn't imagine what he saw in it."

Then her husband suggested she try running a bit longer — say, three miles instead of one. She said, "That three miles — which took me about 30 minutes — must have put me past the 'addiction point,' because from then on I was hooked. I loved running." She has since run several marathons.

This is why I say the sooner you make a habit of going well beyond 20 minutes a day, the better you'll feel. I recommend a *half-hour* of movement, every day from day one on, even if you have to walk all or most or some of it.

Loosely fit that half-hour of movement into a full hour you've blocked out for yourself. Use the extra time to dress slowly for the run-walk, stretch your muscle a bit if you're the type who likes extra exercise, take a leisurely shower or bath after the run, or simply sit down and do some unhurried thinking or talking.

Make your hour a sacred one. Give half of it to activity, half to inactivity, and don't hurry through either one. Get away from the props and demands of civilization — the cars, TVs, newspapers, jobs — and be primitive for awhile. Get away by yourself or with a small group of friends who choose to be with each other, and make this your most creative time.

As long as I've dropped the word "primitive," I may as well go further with it. Primitive runners — animals and people who still must run to eat and avoid being eaten — never run at full-speed for more than a few yards. They seldom run long distances without rest stops. Yet by loping along, then walking, then loping some more, then sprinting for a short stretch to run down their prey, then eating it and sleeping off the effort and the meal, they can go all day without wearing down.

The lesson, though, has been lost on modern runners — whose gods are speed and continuous running effort, both of which are unnatural.

I used to time myself every day over measured courses, and keep track of the records. As times got faster and I had to work harder to beat them, every day's run became a race. Finally, my legs broke down. Nature was telling me something, and I started listening only when I had no choice but to slow down.

I exchanged "faster" for "longer," and made it a point of pride never to stop during a run. If I drank, it was on the run — running in place at water fountains if necessary. If I hit a red stoplight that couldn't be run because of traffic, I'd do laps around the light post. If my shoelaces came undone, I'd let them flap.

Then my legs started breaking down again. They couldn't take the unbroken distance any more than the unbroken speed.

Dr. Ernst van Aaken finally convinced me of this. He's a German who trains everyone from beginners to world record-holders, using mostly comfortably paced running mixed with walking breaks.

Van Aaken says, "Run as a child runs. Run playfully for 5-10 kilometers (3-6 miles) a day, without pain or fatigue. The plan is the same for everyone from competing athletes to men recovering from heart attacks. Only the pace and the amount of walking varies."

The distances sound massive to a beginner. But the walking breaks put them within reach. They allow children who wouldn't run a single mile continuously to cover several miles without tiring during a morning's play.

The same walks allow unconditioned or underconditioned adults to go far beyond their imagined limits. Take Kenneth Crutchlow, for instance. Crutchlow is an English adventurer who once ran from Los Angeles to San Francisco — a distance of almost 500 miles — in 10 days.

When I interviewed Ken, I asked him the kind of preparation he'd done.

"Oh," he said, "none at all. I wouldn't do any special training. That would take the sport out of it. The challenge to me was to do this totally unprepared—as any man on the street might."

"Yes, I see," I said. "But this is incredible. How can you run 50 miles a day for 10 days straight? Trained runners can't even do that kind of mileage."

"You want to know my secret? I don't hurry, and I don't run very far at one time — only a mile or so, and then I walk for awhile. Then I run some more and walk again. It takes me the whole bloody day. But I get there."

Crutchlow had never heard of van Aaken. He had never studied the primitive tribes of Africa or the animals of the wilds. He ran by intuition, which told him to take breaks as he needed them.

I'm telling you to do the same thing. Take walks. Walk the whole bloody way if you want. You may have to walk before you can run. And even after you're running, use walks to extend distances while holding pain and fatigue at bay.

The distances I'm talking about in the suggested beginning program which follows are quite modest compared to those of Crutchlow. The idea is not for you to bull through them but to do them comfortably, and still be able and anxious to run another day.

I'm giving an eight-week starting plan with my ideas of what the specifics should be, just so you'll have a definite plan to go by. You'll develop your own ideas and will modify the plan as you go, and I encourage this.

I choose eight weeks because it seems to be a basic conditioning unit. Marathon runners use it as their building period before a race, upping their mileage for two months. It seems to take that long to adapt thoroughly to new loads.

Look at yourself before you start. Are you in any kind of shape? Do you use your legs regularly — walking, bicycling, playing running games? If you answer no, you need some preliminary walking — only walking — before doing any running.

Are you significantly overweight? Is your 20th birthday a distant memory? Do you tire easily and get winded during moderate exercise? Do you smoke? Do old leg injuries ever bother you? If you say yes to any of these, start by walking.

Walk a steady half-hour or more every day. Test your reactions to it. Even this may be too much, and you may have to cut it back. You may never be able to or want to go beyond the half-hour daily walks. That's okay. This is enough to give most of the same benefits as running, and it's a lot better than the nothing you were doing.

Once you can work up to an hour of steady walking, you're probably ready to add easy running. In fact, I'll advise even those who think they're fit to start with an hour's walk as a test. If it's exhausting, back up to the walking program. If the hour is comfortable, go ahead into the eight-week running build-up.

The eight weeks can be completed in two, or they might take a year to work through. It's up to you because only you are keeping score. You shouldn't hurry because you have a lifetime of running ahead. On the other hand, there's no reason to hold yourself back if you feel ready to charge ahead. Go at your own pace.

The pace shouldn't leave you breathless. Run at a pace which lets you sing or whistle to yourself, or talk normally with a friend. Mix in the amount of walking needed to keep it comfortable.

Go anywhere and everywhere — streets, parks, tracks, whatever you have available. Anyplace you can walk, you can run.

Buy a substantial pair of running shoes if you don't already have some. It's an investment in safety and comfort, the only major money outlay you have in this activity. Other than the special shoes, any light, loose-fitting clothing will do.

Wear a watch to measure your running-walking. Don't check distances! For now, only time counts, not distance. You don't want to combine the two, because the temptation to race with yourself is too strong.

The amount of running should grow as you grow, while the amount of walking shrinks. But the basic system stays the same throughout the eight weeks—and can stay the same forever.

The system involves waves of effort — long runs followed by short ones, then average length, then short again, and so on. "Average" is just that, an average of the week's run. "Long" is twice the average. "Short" is half of average.

The typical weekly pattern:
>   Day one — "active rest" (walk only)
>   Day two — short run
>   Day three — average run
>   Day four — short run
>   Day five — average run
>   Day six — short run
>   Day seven — long run

First Week
>   Day one — walk half-hour.

Days two, four, six — walk 6 minutes, run 1 minute, repeat for half-hour.

Days three, five, seven — walk 15 minutes, run 5 minutes (insert walking breaks as needed) — walk 10 minutes.

Second Week

Day one — walk half-hour.

Days two, four, six — walk 5 minutes, run 1 minute, repeat for half-hour.

Days three, five — walk 15 minutes, run 5 minutes (walk as needed), walk 10 minutes.

Day seven — walk 10 minutes, run 10 minutes (walk as needed), walk 10 minutes.

Third Week

Day one — walk half-hour.

Days two, four, six — walk 4 minutes, run 1 minute, repeat for half-hour.

Days three, five — walk 10 minutes, run 7-8 minutes (walk as needed), walk 12-13 minutes.

Day seven — walk 10 minutes, run 15 minutes (walk as needed), walk 5 minutes.

Fourth Week

Day one — walk half-hour.

Days two, four, six — walk 3 minutes, run 1 minute, repeat for half-hour.

Days three, five — walk 10 minutes, run 10 minutes (walk as needed), walk 10 minutes.

Day seven — walk 5 minutes, run 20 minutes (walk as needed), walk 5 minutes.

Fifth Week

Day one — walk half-hour.

Days two, four, six — walk 2 minutes, run 1 minute, repeat for half-hour.

Days three, five — walk 5 minutes, run 20 minutes (walk as needed), walk 5 minutes.

Day seven — run 30 mins* (walk as needed).

Sixth Week
Day one — walk half-hour.

Days two, four, six — walk 2 minutes, run 1 minute, repeat for half-hour.

Days three, five — walk 5 minutes, run 20 minutes (walk as needed), walk 5 minutes.

Day seven — run 40 minutes* (walk as needed).

Seventh Week
Day one — walk half-hour.

Days two, four, six — walk 2 minutes, run 1 minute, repeat for half-hour.

Days three, five — walk 2-3 minutes, run 25 minutes (walk as needed), walk 2-3 minutes.

Day seven — run 50 minutes* (walk as needed).

Eighth Week
Day one — walk half-hour.

Days two, four, six — walk 1 minute, run 1 minute, repeat for half-hour.

Days three, five — run 30 minutes* (walk as needed).

Day seven — run 60 minutes* (walk as needed).

(*Although no pre-run and post-run walking is listed on these days, it is suggested that you loosen up and cool down by walking for several minutes.)

4. Continuing

One thing both the missionaries of exercise and the haters of it don't understand: Long-time runners run for many different reasons, but almost never because it's good for them. It may or may not be a panacea for healthful living. But that doesn't seem to be important any more. It may have been at the start, but not now.

I was running with a 50-year-old named John. He said, "I started running — as almost everyone else did — after reading Kenneth Cooper's *Aerobics*. A very inspirational and in some ways very frightening book. I guess I needed words that strong to get me moving."

Cooper says, in so many worlds, "run (or swim, or walk, or cycle) or you'll die." It's a negative emphasis, and an effective one. For a while. But as the fear wears off the cure may seem worse than the ailment if a more positive reason for running hasn't developed.

Lately, doctors like Meyer Friedman have said the "cure" is worse than taking nothing. His statistics sound impressive if you don't read them closely. Two or three joggers in every hundred thousand have died of heart attacks. Therefore, he concludes, it's dangerous for everyone.

Cooper's implication is "run or die." Friedman's message is "run *and* die." Which to believe?

Neither, says my friend John: "After I'd been running a few months, I found there were better, more positive reasons for doing it than losing weight and protecting myself from a heart attack. The psychological satisfaction — a 'feel good' feeling, so to speak — is much more immediate, certain and dramatic than anything I might or might not get sometime in the future."

John said if he'd believed all the promises and run only because of them, and hadn't lost a pound or had ended up in a cardiac care unit, he would have felt a bit cheated. As is, "If someone proved tomorrow, without a doubt, that there was no physical benefit whatsoever in running — and in fact that it has harmful side-effects — I would keep right on doing it without a second thought."

The only people to be weeded out by such a discovery would be the ones who were running for the least of all reasons, anyway. Running only to exercise the muscles is like eating only to work the jaws or having sex only to train the pelvis. Those things happen, but so much more is going on that you don't take time to notice. The exercise may be good for you, but it would be just as much fun even if it weren't. Maybe more.

On the whole, the running scene is a lot better place to be now than it was 10 or 20 years ago. Runners on the streets are a common enough sight to be ignored now, and that's good. I don't mind if people think I'm crazy. It only bothers me when they yell it at me. And that doesn't happen much any more.

But as running has become respectable, something has gone out of it — something I can't quite describe. It switched over sometime during the late 1960s or early 1970s from being a vice to a virtue. People began thinking runners might not be so weird after all. Doctors began talking up the physical benefits.

Runners who had come to this sport because it was different, because it set them apart from the crowd, because this was a secret pleasure, found they had lots of company. And these new people — most of them, anyway; at first, anyway — looked at running differently. It wasn't fun. It wasn't something they'd do for nothing because they enjoyed it. They did it because it was supposed to be good for them. They took it as a duty, like a medicine.

The doctors who made running respectable told us everything about what it does for us, but little about what keeps us doing it.

One sure way to kill a trend is to make a fad of it. Because as sure as something comes into style, it will soon be out. It happened in recent years with everything from hula-hoops to anti-war protests. It happens every year with hem lengths and rock music preferences.

On the other hand, a sure way to breathe new life into an activity is to rule it immoral or illegal or unhealthy. Give it a forbidden-fruit flavor. Attach a risk to it, and the taste is enhanced.

At the time when preachers dealing with virtue are having a hard time filling their pews and collection plates, peddlers of vice are growing rich.

Despite the anti-smoking campaigns, cigarette sales were never better. Despite groups like the WCTU and AA, alcoholic drinks increasingly fuel the country. Consumption of illegal drugs and illicit sex are up. So is the use of white flour and sugar, which the natural foods people call poison.

Everyone talks about the dangers of eating too much, but no one does anything about it. Everyone talks about how they really should start exercising — tomorrow.

Everyone knows what's good for them, but puts off doing it because it doesn't sound like any fun.

So maybe what we should do is change our tactics in promoting running. Instead of saying it's the exercise everyone must take or rot in hell, we should preach *against* it.

Stand up and say, "Brothers and sisters, don't be tempted by the ways of the flesh. Don't be taken in by the sensuous delights of distance running. Resist! Cut out this devil which leads you into temptation." And your listeners will suddenly wonder what they're missing.

Good intentions may make you feel pure of heart. You may feel proud of your sacrifices as you do your physical penance. Good intentions are said to pave the way to the hot place, but in this case they more often lead nowhere at all. That's because people soon tire of doing what they don't want, and they let it slip quietly away. It may have lasted two days, maybe a month. But when the good work is gone, it's usually gone forever.

So instead of treating running as a sterile act of virtue, look on it as something of a vice. Seek out its wickedness. Do it for its excitement and daring.

Take the attitude that you're running against the currents of conventional thought and action — which is true even now, when running is generally tolerated. It's still accepted for what it gives, not for what it is — for the results, not for the process.

If anyone asks, "What are you running for?" answer, "Nothing."

If he says, "Where are you going?" tell him, "Nowhere."

And if he wonders, "Then why do you run," you say, "I don't run to go anyplace, but just to go."

These kinds of answers will certify you as different. Yet they are the best reasons to run and the best ways to keep running. These answers will convince your friends and your family that your running is a destructive habit. And that's good, because nothing is harder to break than a bad habit.

Of course I don't view running as a bad habit. I only exaggerate to make a point. That is, running at its best is play — done for no other reason than that it is fun. Not fun in the ha-ha sense, but fun in a quietly satisfying way. To run only for practical ends is to make work of it, to make it a duty instead of something you want to do and would do for nothing.

"Work," wrote Mark Twain, "is whatever the body is obliged to do. Play is whatever it is not obliged to do."

George Sheehan, the runners' conscience, says, "When we expose play to the function of promoting fitness and preventing heart attacks, we change its gold to dross... What we need is to conserve those mysterious and elusive elements of play which make it its *own* reward. We must remove anything that suggests practicality and usefulness. What we do must be fun and impractical and useless, or else we won't do it.

"We should be in sports not because they are practical but because they are not, not because we feel better but because we don't care how we feel, not because our fitness is increased but because we're so interested we don't even notice.

"If we become fit and impervious to heart attacks and all those other dread diseases, it will be because we don't care if we drop dead doing what we like to do."

Of course Sheehan doesn't expect anyone to drop dead while running. He exaggerates, too, to make his point. He's a doctor as well as a runner, so he knows what running does for us physically. He sees every day that it leads to health and vitality and all the rest of it. But he emphasizes that this is a *by-product*, not a goal. There's little doubt that good health comes with exercise, but when our exercise is play this happens almost incidentally. We're too occupied with the activity to notice the good things going on inside because of it.

Dr. Sheehan again: "Exercise that is drudgery, labor, something done only for the final result, is a waste of time. If I hated to run, and ran only for longevity and was killed by a truck after five years at the sport, I would have a right to shake my fist at whoever advised it."

You'd be even more put out if you'd been promised a heart-disease-free or cancer-free or ulcers- or hemorrhoids-free future and these symptoms developed. Which they do. Even in runners.

So don't be disappointed. Don't run because it will be good for you later, but because it feels good to do while you're at it. If running is not and can never be your play, find another game.

The people who keep running are normal individuals who treat their runs as normal parts of their day. Running, in other words, is their habit. These are not ascetics who take their pleasure in self-sacrifice. Their running is a plus, not a minus. They are not masochists who take delight in pain. Like any normal person, they do what gives pleasure and avoid the painful. They only wade through occasional, temporary, mild pain to get to the pleasure on the other side.

Look at me. I've been running for all of my adolescent and adult life. I've been through my share of pain, but never because I liked suffering. I like what goes with it. That's all. And there has been a hundred times more of the "what goes with it" than pain.

Basically, I'm a cowardly, weak-willed man. I'm afraid to argue with anyone, petrified by the thought of a dentist's drill or a doctor's needle, and I regularly detour around unpleasant work. I'm tempted by the pleasures of the flesh. Rich, sweet foods. Evenings in front of the TV. Long nights in a warm bed.

My wife must bribe me to carry out the garbage, feed the cats and mow the yard because I'd rather be reading a book or taking a nap. I'm lazy. But I still run 4-8 miles a day and 12-15 on Saturdays — partly because I've always done it and don't know any other way to start the day, and partly because it lets me be lazier and more self-indulgent when I'm not running.

I have a theory about this. It may be all wet, but it's a theory I'll cling to until someone proves it wrong. I think because we run, runners can get by with a lot of things that non-runners can't.

For instance, we can overeat and it doesn't show. I weigh 130 pounds, and have to eat as much as a non-runner twice my size just to keep my weight up. More than just quantity, though, runners are allowed to cheat on quality. The fuels for this kind of effort are carbohydrate and fat. Most so-called "junk foods" are starchy and fatty. I consume Dr Pepper, butter brickle ice cream and tortilla chips with sour cream dip at a rate which would alarm nutritionists. But it doesn't worry me because I know it will burn up the next morning. If it isn't there to burn, I feel weak.

I don't drink alcohol, but that's part of my Bible Belt upbringing. Most runners do drink. Some crave it to the extent that their runs are little more than an excuse for the beer they pop open afterwards.

Walter Stack, a runner in his late 60s from San Francisco, doesn't wait till after. He drinks beer during — at the rate of a can every four or five miles. Walt goes through a six-pack during a marathon.

Stack also knows a morning run is the greatest cure for a hangover. "The first few miles are miserable as hell," he says, "but as soon as the oxygen starts rushing through your blood and pushing the crap out, you feel like living again."

Since I don't drink, I don't know how bad hangovers can be. But they can't be much worse than waking up too early after going to bed too late.

I like my sleep. I grew up a farmer's son, and picked up a habit of going to bed with the sun and staying under the covers for 8-10 hours. That habit is still with me.

If I'm not in bed by 10, I feel it the next morning at six. My mouth tastes like a garbage truck drove through and was leaking. My eyes are nearly cemented shut by what my daughter calls "sleepy bugs." My thinking is tangled up in cobwebs.

The last thing I want to do is run. But I know from experience it's the first thing I need. It doesn't make sense — working hard to feel less tired — but somehow it works.

As with Walt Stack's hangover, the first couple of miles are miserable. I feel like I'm waking up from a nightmare, stumbling along in the dark and cold without knowing where I am or why I'm there.

But then oxygen starts to do its job. It pries open my eyes, rushes in through my nose and mouth, and saturates the blood, which goes racing into every corner carrying a transfusion of energy. Before long, sights and thoughts are coming into focus. I see the day may be worth facing after all.

I'm not urging anyone to dissipate freely or not to dissipate at all. What I am saying is that it isn't necessary to be a fanatic about health habits.

Chronic cheating is no good. Eventually it will catch up with you, as the traffic cops do to people who regularly jump stoplights and zip along 10 miles per hour above the limit. But if you only occasionally fall off the wagon and eat too much, drink too freely or sleep too little, running will probably neutralize the distress.

In other words, no one has to give up all bad habits to be a runner. No one has to ask, "Is this good for me?" a hundred times a day.

Running is a neutralizer of bad habits. But in a much more positive sense, it is a catalyst which makes good things happen. It doesn't require any special attention, and in fact works better without it. Take care of the running, and everything else seems to take care of itself.

5. Curing

Some doctors say running is a panacea. For instance, a southern California faction of the American Medical Joggers Association headed by Dr. Thomas Bassler says running six miles a day and finishing marathons is absolute protection against heart disease.

Bassler writes, "So far, true marathoners — those who can complete the 26.2 miles — appear to be immune to coronary heart disease (CHD). We have yet to find a marathoner at any age with fatal CHD. There is no evidence that speed protects but mileage does. It is safe to say that a hobby marathoner who finishes a four-hour marathon has at least six years of CHD protection."

At the other extreme are Dr. Meyer Friedman and Dr. Ray Rosenman, who say that running is a form of "mass suicide" with no redeeming qualities, either physically or spiritually.

Not surprisingly, Bassler is a marathoner; Friedman and Rosenman have never run. Doctors have their prejudices, too.

I prefer to hear from doctors who run but are cautious in their praise of it. Dr. Peter Wood is one. He is not an M.D. but a Ph.D. in biochemistry doing research at Stanford University on the effects of exercise. He began running in his native England more than 40 years ago.

"Perhaps 50,000 miles later," he says, "I am still at it. It all adds up to a lot of races on several continents, lot of friends and a lot of travel. But most of all, a lot of time. What if I'd invested that time in writing novels? Would I be famous? Suppose I'd covered those 50,000 miles on foot selling encyclopedias? Would I be wealthy? Has it all been worth it?"

Dr. Wood leaves no doubt that it has: "My views on this subject come from the literature, from studies that we have conducted as part of the Stanford Heart Disease Prevention Program, and of course from my personal bias — all 40 years of which I try rather unsuccessfully to suppress."

He was, after all, running long before he was a scientist studying running. And though he studies the physical effects, he says the psychological ones are "probably the most beneficial... Runners clearly see that powerful forces are at work, many of which seem to act to their advantage. We know how relaxed and at peace with the world most runners are at the end of a hard run."

One Stanford study Wood was involved with examined 45 distance runners, ages 35-65. The most comforting finding was that these men had physical profiles normally associated with people half their age. Endurance, naturally, was extraordinary. Weight was typically that of a 20-year-old, though most of these runners were in their 40s.

This is normally a heart-attack-prone age, and high levels of the fats called triglycerides and cholesterol in the blood stream are suspected causes. Triglycerides in the runners were half of the norm for their age group. Cholesterol counts didn't appear to be affected very much by running, but Dr. Wood's team found in the runners a different *type* of cholesterol — small, relatively innocuous particles.

Wood says, "The cholesterol picture for our older male runners was very much like that for young women (who have the lowest incidence of heart disease)."

In fact, the doctor notes, in his 40 years of running he has seen only one heart accident during a race — where something like this would seem most likely to happen.

"True," he says, "such tragedies are dramatic and often publicized in newspapers. But I am not aware of good data indicating that running carries an increased risk of such events. The vast majority continue to occur, unpublicized, in bed or seated."

The question, though, is this: Are these people as healthy as they are because they run? Or do they run because they are this healthy?

It's a little of both. I've seen fat men become thin with running, sick ones become well, weak ones become strong. But I've also seen a hell of a lot of people start running and stop before the first month is out because they can't stand the pain of it. They get injured or they simply can't face any more running. There's a kind of Darwinian natural selection process going on. "Survival of the fittest," if you wish.

Two men begin running together, for instance. They are neighbors, Fred and Larry. Fred is heavy. He weighs 40 pounds more than he did on high school graduation day, 15 years ago. And he smokes a pack and a half of cigarettes a day. His only exercise has been a round of golf every weekend or two. It's a social event as much as an athletic one.

Larry is the same age and is Fred's golf partner. That's his only formal exercise, but he plays more out of duty than desire. Larry prefers to take his long walks by himself without ruining them by chasing a white ball. It infuriates

Fred that every spoonful of food he eats turns directly into fat, while Larry can eat all he wants without gaining weight. Larry doesn't smoke.

Fred huffs and puffs through two weeks of running, dreading every step. Then his ankles and knees grow sore, and he's silently happy because it gives him a ready excuse to drop this boring exercise.

Meanwhile, Larry goes on. He finds that he likes running even better now that he's alone. His mileage and pace pick up. He quits playing golf on the weekends.

Fred is worse off than before. He not only isn't getting much exercise, but the thought of it is more distasteful than ever. Larry is the healthier of the two because he runs. But we can't ignore the fact that he was able to keep running because he was healthier at the start.

There exists a "natural runner" and a "running life-style" even in persons who never take a running step. The runner's physique is naturally lean, built for endurance and not strength-speed. The physiologists call this an ectomorphic somatotype.

The natural runner has a loner personality. He's happiest in solitary pursuits—working alone, reading books, that kind of thing. He's more excited about ideas than by material possessions. He appears to be something of an ascetic because his appetites aren't strong.

The natural runner is a "flee-er," not a fighter. He has an instinct for survival whilch depends on his brains and his feet, not on his muscle.

The natural runner lives a running life-style because he's comfortable with it. He eats regularly and moderately, and drinks little or nothing with alcohol in it. He doesn't smoke. He makes sure he gets the sleep he needs. Even if

61

he doesn't run, he likes lonely physical activity like walking or bicycling or gardening, and he does it almost every day. He lives this way because he's most comfortable with regularity and moderation.

The natural runner isn't usually a compulsive worrier about his health, but he's healthy because he lives the way he does. It's an almost unconscious part of his survival instinct. This is his way of building the endurance to keep going when his mesomorphic and endomorphic friends are dropping out.

Three things decide how long and how well we live, and only one of them can we do much about.

One is *what* we're given to live with. "Heredity," in other words. We inherit tendencies toward health and illness with the parents we choose.

Two is *where* we live — "environment." It would be nice to choose a home in the clear, thin mountain air or on the quiet of the farm away from the rat race. But few of us can live so well.

Three is *how* we live with the inherited tools and the surroundings. Call it "life-style." Here, there are lots of life-giving choices which we can make every day.

In 1975, a team of California researchers concluded that people who regularly practiced seven Golden Rules of health could add 7-11 years to their lives. Dr. Lester Breslow of the UCLA School of Public Health said, "The daily habits of people have a great deal more to do with what makes them sick and when they die than all the influences of medicine."

The seven rules:

1. *No smoking.*
2. *Maintain normal weight.*

3. *Eat regularly and not between meals.*
4. *Eat breakfast.*
5. *Sleep eight hours a night.*
6. *Drink (alcohol) only moderately.*
7. *Exercise regularly.*

Dr. Breslow added, "A man of 55 who follows all seven good health habits has the same physical status as a person 25-30 years younger who follows less than two of the health practices." He probably figures alcohol is the last thing a person will give up, and that exercise is the last thing one will begin. So he puts them sixth and seventh on his list.

Exercise is at the bottom, but that isn't to imply it's least important. Dr. Nedra Belloc of the California Health Department, who worked with Breslow, said, "In our study, the men who reported that they engaged in active sports had the lowest mortality — just half that experienced by men who reported they only sometimes gardened or exercised."

Presumably, the exercisers survived even better than those who never did anything more physical than open a car door. But, nothing was said about them — possibly because no one would admit to doing nothing.

Running wasn't mentioned by name, but no doubt it is included among the "active sports." There is strong evidence that running keeps the plumbing cleared, like a regular Roto-Rooter treatment. This has a lot to do with health and longevity. And there is strong evidence to show that running acts indirectly on most of the other good health habits which Dr. Breslow lists.

Runners don't even have to try very hard to live this way. Everything sort of falls into line naturally. People who normally don't have the will to give up a cigarette, an extra helping of dessert or a third martini before dinner — for the sake of their health — find themselves detouring around habits which interfere with their running performance.

Runners almost never smoke, for example, because the damage from lung pollution is too obvious. Dr. Peter Wood of Stanford says, "Our sample of 45 older runners contained not a single smoker (although the average number of smokers of similar age is 38 percent). However, several of them had smoked at one time when not running."

Runner's World surveyed its readers several years ago and found similar results. Only one runner in 500 was a smoker, though 20 percent had smoked regularly before taking up the sport.

The non-smoking habit, says Dr. Wood, immediately gives runners "an enormous health advantage, since the evidence linking smoking to cancer, heart disease and emphysema is now overwhelming."

Evidence is equally strong that obesity — gross overweight — is a drag on health. And fatness and fitness can't coexist. There is no such thing as a fat fit runner. Adult runners carry 10 percent less fat than inactive, "normal" people their age.

"Everyone knows that exercise burns fat," says Peter Wood. "But it takes up to 50 miles of running to burn one pound. Less well known is the fact that vigorous exercise regulates the appetite. This is probably the runner's secret. He manages to adjust caloric intake very nicely so that he neither wastes away nor becomes overweight. He has a perfectly operating 'appestat.'"

Alcohol is, in Wood's words, "an interesting subject." A high percentage of runners drink it, he says, "but I know of no runners who drink it obsessively." In other words, runners seem better able to judge their limits.

Perhaps, too, the doctor adds, "the harmful effects of excess alcohol are ameliorated by vigorous activity."

"Live like a marathoner." These are the guiding words of the running doctors who make up the American Medical Joggers Association. They de-emphasize the "don'ts" which most doctors prescribe for patients, and which few patients follow. Instead, the AMJA gives one central "do." Do endurance activity.

The group's chief theoretician and missionary, Dr. Thomas Bassler of Los Angeles, says, "This motto — 'Live like a marathoner so you can run like one' — motivates more (patients) than the usual admonitions about smoking and diet."

Bassler is the pathologist who says he has yet to see a heart attack death among runners who regularly do at least six miles and have finished the marathon. The claim is disputed by more conservative doctors.

However, Bassler contends, "The health benefits of the marathoning life-style will become increasingly evident as larger numbers take up the sport."

Peter Wood notes that the U.S. heart-attack death rate in recent years has actually dropped after years of steady climbing. He says the new attention to endurance activity "just might be one of the factors in this drop."

Tom Bassler concludes that "diseases which account for two-thirds of the deaths in the average population are not expected to show up in those who are actively marathoning. I do not expect to see distance runners die from heart attack, cancer of the lungs, emphysema, cirrhosis of the liver due to hardening of the arteries. All of these diseases require a life-style that would interfere with running performance."

AMJA President Dr. Ron Lawrence adds, "I am convinced that running extends life. But even if it didn't add a single day to a person's life, it would be worth doing because running clearly enhances the quality of life.

"First, if you stick with it a year, you're hooked. Running's addictive. Second, it changes your whole life-style. Nobody's ever the same again. Running produces tranquility. We know it changes a Type A personality to a Type B. You get away from the rat race on a regular basis."

There's more: "You quit smoking in order to run long distance. Your consumption of alcohol drops for the same reason. You simply have more fun if smoking and drinking don't slow you down. Eating habits change because good nutrition is an integral part of aerobic exercise. Your total well-being improves. You sleep better but require less sleep. Your sex life is enhanced. Anxieties decrease, and you're better prepared to cope with stress. Work productivity improves. You get away from the television and begin seeing a new world around you."

Running is the catalyst. You get so hooked on it and so interested in doing it each day that you barely notice the protection it's building for tomorrow.

6. Calming

Running is a pursuit of happiness.

A few lucky people can find calm contentment sitting down. The ones who meditate say this is true for them. But most of us won't take the time to learn and practice meditation in the traditional form of sitting quietly and clearing our heads for a half-hour to an hour a day.

Some people are meditators by nature. They're probably the ones who need it the least anyway, since they're already rather mellow of personality if they're willing to sit still that long.

Those of us who are like hyperactive nine-year-olds won't sit and wait for happiness to come to us, so we must find it in a way which better suits our personalities—by chasing after it.

There is happiness in the pursuit—enough of it not only to tranquilize us against the everyday tensions and anxieties of a neurotic world, but also to help correct certain types of severely disturbed behavior.

Movement is strong medicine. Later, I'll tell of some cases which show just how strong it is. But first let me make some tentative stabs at why it works as it does.

1. *Running is a "survival mechanism."* That's the description Dr. William Glasser uses in his book *Positive Addiction*. He says, "This need to run is programmed genetically into our brains."

Our ancestors reacted to threats in one of two ways: by preparing to stand their ground and fight, or preparing to get the hell out of the danger area. Either way, their body's resources were marshaled for action.

Man still faces threats. In a crowded, fast-paced environment, he faces more than his ancestors did. Since modern living offers so much tension and so few chances for socially acceptable fights, man gets his release by fleeing.

2. *Running relaxes an overtensed body.* Dr. Paul Insel and Dr. Walton Roth of Stanford University say, "The most profound muscular and mental relaxation cannot be achieved by just trying to relax. The deepest relaxation, as measured by electrodes inserted in the muscles, follows a period of voluntary *increased* muscle tension."

3. *Running relaxes an overstimulated mind.* Everyone needs some time every day to "spin-out," says Dr. William Glasser. Free-floating thinking, day-dreaming, fantasizing are important to mental health. Glasser's advice is to "program ourselves less than we do. We should allow for time off, some leeway, some slack in the day. Never make it too tight."

Simply the time spent running—without TV, radio, newspapers, books to fill the thoughts—is mind cleansing.

4. *Running is "meditation on the move."* Running and transcendental meditation are two of the most popular self-improvement methods of the 1970s. And their similarities in techniques and results are striking.

In *Tranquility Without Pills,* Jhan Robins and David Fisher write, "TM acts to remove tension, frustration and worry. The entire process is based on the fact that man stores his feelings of stress inside himself, and this stress forces him to act in certain—often anti-social—ways. Through meditation, these pockets of stress are released, which enables meditators to enjoy a much freer, much more fulfilled life than they previously did."

Substitute the word "running" for "TM" and "runner" for "meditator," and the rest of that paragraph holds up as written.

5. *Running produces hormone changes.* A British medical team headed by Dr. Malcolm Carruthers reported that the hormone norepinephrine (another name for adrenaline) is "the chemical basis for happy feelings." They said as little as 10 minutes of suitable (endurance) exercise will double the body's level of this hormone, destroying depression— and the effect is long-lasting.

Dr. Kenneth Cooper noted in late 1975, "There have been some interesting studies recently showing such things as the metabolism of thyroid hormones is different in a person who is exercising." This may have something to do with the good feelings one has during and immediately after running, and why we feel bad when we can't run.

"There are many things that occur," Cooper added, "that we don't even know yet."

The fact is, however, that running does its good work whether we know it or not. I'm not so concerned with *why* it works as *that* it does.

Richard Willis is a former inmate at the California State Mental Hospital for the Criminally Insane. We've exchanged several letters, the last coming from him in late 1975 when he wrote:

"Fortunately for me—and I hope for society too—I'll be going home soon. And it's about time as far as I'm concerned. This doesn't mean I will carry any bitterness with me. Quite the contrary. Fact is, I've learned a lot, accomplished a lot, meditated a lot and generally enjoyed life a lot during this last incarceration."

Earlier, Richard had traced his history for me. "I was a very straight kid through school, very square, real insecure. . . . I stumbled into cross-country the fall of my junior year. As fate had it, I was pretty good in the running department (4:24 mile). As I entered my local junior college, distance running seemed to be my only interest, the only activity in which I could earn good strokes for myself.

"Then I broke my leg in a motorcycle accident. After getting out of the hospital and surviving a case of severe depression, I juggled my plans and classes around. Before I knew it, I was an aspiring actor, with a typical dream of one day becoming a superstar. To match the outward flow of fate, my personality had made a momentous change. All of a sudden, I was super-outgoing, with plenty of attention coming my way.

"I moved to Hollywood to take the town by storm. Or so I thought. All the while, my once-beloved running shoes had taken a seat in the back row. I was superficially messing around with various occult philosophies. I went through a couple of heavy hallucinations without any use of drugs, tripping from time to time down the delusional byways of life.

"Before I knew it, I was an apartment burglar, stealing for the pure sensation of the activity, thoroughly enjoying myself while thinking that what I was doing was completely okay within the divine scheme of things. I mean, I was having a lot of fun ripping people off.

70

"After about 100 burglaries, I finally got caught stealing a lamp, a dirty beach towel and a boomerang. I turned over my secret garage to the cops, giving up the estimated $70,000 worth of other people's belongings."

Willis was in and out of prison and mental institutions during the next several years before winding up at Atascadero, which he calls "the grand-daddy of mental hospitals." He wrote to me in July 1975.

"A strong and serious dozen of us run between 30 and 120 miles each week around our beloved asphalt rectangles—330 yards, encircled by walls high enough to give Steve Smith a hearty challenge— a track which heats up just like an oven most of the year.

"Besides boasting of our physical health, a few of us Dinky-Rink Oven Runners run for our sanity—that is to say our mental health actually depends upon the virtues of the distance running habit.

"I personally have been insane two times too often, raising enough cane in society to become an unpopular fellow with the law. And for a while there, it seemed that only heavy medication could keep me mellow and 'in contact,' though sedating me into robot status in the process.

"But fortunately, I have managed to rekindle an old desire for distance running, and as a result my cardiovascular workouts have replaced all of my need for medication. Though our distance running endeavors go virtually unrecognized by the hospital administration, for their therapeutic values, those of us who enjoy running daily in the Oven know better."

Kenneth Fox was an alcoholic. He tells how he overcame that addiction.

"Once, a neurotically disturbed friend of mine—a non-alcoholic—described her emotional feelings to me. She said it is as if you are suffering from intense pain, but there is nowhere physically that you can locate the pain.

"One day several years ago, while almost blindly fleeing the emotional pain of alcoholism, I ran as far as I could (perhaps a mile or two). Later, during withdrawal, I ran again to escape the pain I could not locate. Each time I ran, the pain subsided. As the pain of withdrawal grew, so did the intensity of my 'therapy.'

"Years later, secure and casual in my avoidance of alcohol, running 40-50 miles per week, I look back in amazement at my apparent good luck at having started running when I did. A pastime which I would have thought I was initiating primarily for physical health reasons has become the most emotionally stabilizing factor in my life.

"Quitting is forever, or it makes little sense. And for the recovering alcoholic, the notion of an indefinite future of abstinence is so devastating emotionally that he is cautioned to face life one day at a time. It is apparent to me now that my recovery was made possible by the psychological benefits of running.

"The climb up from alcoholism is no picnic. I list four requirements to assure a successful ascent. To begin, there must be discipline. The recovering alcoholic must constantly wrestle with a demon within himself which awaits its chance to ensnare him. Second, there must be a change of life-style, a change to new activities and new pastimes to forget and supplant the prior life. Third, there must be a new form of relaxation to replace social drinking to which the alcoholic has become so accustomed, and which he will continually be barraged with opportunities to resume. Fourth, and most permanent, the recovering alcoholic needs a new personality, a new image to which he can aspire—contrary to and in conflict with the drinking personality he is leaving behind.

"It is psychologically much more satisfying to travel to a good place than to leave a bad one. Quitting an addictive habit is in this respect lacking in personal satisfaction. When your heroes invite you to drink one down with them, it is more than a little difficult always to concentrate on that abstract good place to which you are traveling.

"Long distance running represents a definite good place—a haven—which the recovering alcoholic can strive from, the emotionally satisfying image of constructive action which allows him to concentrate upon his goals regardless of any distractions around him.

"When my self-image became intimately associated with my own physical performance and well-being, that image also became antipathetic to the use of alcohol. I can never take a drink again, not as a non-alcoholic. But that fact is of little significance to me since I have no interest in ever taking another drink. I stumbled into a form of therapy which someday medical science will prescribe."

Thaddeus Kostrubala started running to lose weight and to tone up his heart—the same reasons most adults begin exercising. And he had the same surprise most beginners run across after several months. While the activity was doing what he'd hoped for his body (he was on his way to losing 60 pounds), it was doing even more for his head.

This had more than personal significance for Kostrubala because he is the chief of psychiatry at Mercy Hospital in San Diego. He began to experiment with running as a tool in psychotherapy for his patients. Some early results:

— A woman was suffering from anorexia nervosa — meaning she had lost interest in eating and had wasted away to 79 pounds. In 18 months of running therapy, her appetite returned and she gained more than 50 pounds.

— A patient diagnosed as an "unchangeable paranoid schizophrenic" recovered well enough to maintain a B average in college and hold a job. No identifiable traces of his schizophrenia remain, and he needs no medication.

— A severely depressed woman blossomed as an artist.

— A heroin addict freed himself of his habit by replacing it with a more positive one.

Running itself is addictive, says Dr. Kostrubala, if it's done in the way he prescribes. He obviously controls the distance and pace carefully as he runs with mentally disturbed patients. The runs last about an hour, three times a week. The pace is gentle—about three-fourths of maximum heart rate, or roughly 130-150 beats per minute. This is followed immediately by group therapy for up to an hour.

Dr. Kostrubala described his sessions to Frances Caldwell in *The Physician and Sportsmedicine* magazine. "The first 20 or 30 minutes (of a run) you feel rotten, fatigued, shot down. Some in depression will actually cry. The draining feeling is emotional, not physical. That sense of depression disappears after 30 minutes. I've never talked to anyone who maintains that depressed feeling.

"Almost as consistent is the 'runner's high' that occurs 30-40 minutes after starting. It's a distinct euphoria with feelings of excitement and enthusiasm. This is why most of

74

our group runners supplement the dosage with independent running.

"I call the period of 40-60 minutes the 'altered state of consciousness' that must be similar to the catalytic experience of drugs or religion that allows us to alter our lives from within. It's an opening into the unconsciousness.

"The thought process is altered. Problems become irrelevant or annoying, and are let go. And, like some inner consultation, a random jumble of ideas flashes through the field of consciousness.

"That's why it's important to get the group together immediately after the hour run. There's new material waiting to be discussed, evaluated and used. Sometimes the ideas don't make much sense and can be discarded in a rational way. Other times, they've led to new insights into problems."

It's temping here to read too much into these cases. I'm not hinting that running is a mental cure-all, any more than a physical one. Certainly, I'm not suggesting that anyone should attempt self-treatment of serious problems. Get professional help.

What I am suggesting is that if running can help correct such conditions as schizophrenia and heroin addiction, it must be of some value in taking care of everyday stresses and strains. There, we can be our own psychiatrist.

Runner Frank Farwell has written, "I saw my psychiatrist again yesterday. I got all the troubles out of my head. And when I finished, I felt like a new man—at peace with the world, complications of the mind resolved. I stayed in his office about an hour, and it cost me seven cents."

He figures that's how much his shoes and socks depreciated during his hour. This is the runner's only significant expense.

Frank adds, "With a Finnish sauna and pecan pie coming a close second and third, running is the best natural high I know. And at that price, who can complain?"

7. Slowing

TIME.

The name screams out from the cover of the magazine in black capital letters. And a fitting name it is for a journal carrying news to the person in a hurry.

As I rush through the week's issue, three pages — two ads and one article — stop me long enough to think how far a modern epidemic has progressed.

Dr. Meyer Friedman and Dr. Ray Rosenman call it "hurry sickness"—the compulsive drive to do more and more in less and less time. We all suffer from the disease to an extent, because we are forced to live by schedules and deadlines, we live with fast-moving machines which stir up a chronic sense of urgency. We aren't sure where we want to go or if it's worth going there, but we feel we have to get there in a hurry.

The automobile is the main vehicle in this rush, and it is fashionable to blame it for our impatience at the pace with which we move. But perhaps the real tyrants are clocks and watches.

For most of man's history, we couldn't measure time much more accurately than to say, "It's a little while before dawn," or "It's late afternoon." We didn't need to be much more precise than that when we got up at dawn, worked until the sun was straight overhead, stopped for lunch and worked again until dusk.

Then man began playing with time, foolishly thinking that by knowing every minute and second he could manipulate it. He alternately tried to speed it up and slow it down, and succeeded only in shaking up his own bred-in rhythms.

The first clocks were sundials which gave a rough estimate of the time of day by a shadow thrown on a plate. They only worked when the sun was shining.

I'm no authority on the history of timing devices, but I'd guess that the first crude mechanical clocks were something like sundials. The face was divided into hours, and a single hand pointed to the right one.

Then someone split the hour into 60 minutes by adding another hand to the face. Next came a second hand which hurried around the dial once a minute and stopwatches which split the second.

These clocks and watches were all refinements of the old round sundial. You had to work a bit to find the time, looking at three different hands and interpreting them.

Now, hands are disappearing. The new wave in time is the digital readout. These devices have no moving parts, only tiny electronic circuitry. The time in hours, minutes and seconds spells itself out in red or yellow letters against a black background at the push of a button.

The digitals are battery-powered. They never need winding. And their accuracy is incredible. The companies which make them try to outdo each other with accuracy claims. *TIME* advertises a watch guaranteed not to stray by more than a minute per year.

This brings to my mind something Henry David Thoreau said about a hundred years ago when telegraph lines had connected Maine with Texas. Everyone was marveling at what technology had accomplished. Thoreau asked what Maine and Texas possibly could have to say to each other.

My comment when I hear of digital watches which run a race with time and finish within a minute at the end of the year is similar. Why bother? It gets there at exactly the same rate whether we watch it or not. Time doesn't change. But it changes us when we try to bend it.

When we work against time, this innocent rhythm of nature is seen as a competitor, a tyrant. We run a frantic, futile, neurotic race against the precious minute, without seeing it's a race we never can win.

The same issue of *TIME* carried an innocuous ad for men's support stockings. It was the history of a leg, titled "10 Years in the Life of a Man on the Go." But it might have been called "10 Years in the Rat Race" or "10 Years of Hurry Up and Wait" or "10 Years of Frustration." Written on the leg was the story of how it was used.

"Rushing 5336 hours to be on time."
"Standing 8600 hours waiting for appointments."
"Walking 89 miles to and from parking lots."
"Waiting 10,000 minutes in long lines."
"Stepping on the accelerator 16,500 times."
"Stepping on the brakes 72,000 times."
"Running 223 miles to catch a bus, train or plane."

This man and his legs apparently are typical. They spend many hours each day rushing from here to there, then have to stand and fidget when they arrive. The "man on the go" totals less than a mile a day of running and walking—and it is more of the same, a rush to get somewhere.

In this man's full and hectic day, slow and plodding movement is one of the easiest things to eliminate. Is it any wonder, then, that his heart and head are in a race to see which one gives out first?

Suddenly, he notices something giving out. He says to himself, "Exercise! Exercise is supposed to cure anything." And he rushes into it the same way he goes into everything else.

The man on the go wants instant results. He wants his exercise to be quick and relatively painless, like buying lunch of a double cheeseburger, French fries and a large Coke at McDonald's, and gobbling it down in two minutes instead of taking an hour out for a relaxed, more nutritious meal. This man buys books which promise fitness in a hurry. And he helped put Dr. Laurence Morehouse's *Total Fitness in 30 Minutes a Week* on the best-seller list for the better part of 1975.

TIME reviewed the book in the issue I've talked about. The article quoted Dr. Kenneth Cooper, who has for years been America's guru of fitness. His *Aerobics* books, which themselves have sold millions of copies, advocate regular doses of continuous, moderate exercise—preferably running.

Cooper said the exercises recommended in *Total Fitness* aren't adequate to produce his definition of fitness. If the exercise were running, which isn't part of Dr. Morehouse's program, *60* minutes a week might bring a person up to minimum standards. But "total" fitness requires even more work than that.

I obviously side with Cooper in this argument. But not completely. While he has done more to promote running for health than anyone else ever has and I have nothing but praise for his work in general, *Aerobics* has a flaw from my admittedly biased point of view. That is, Dr. Cooper's system puts a premium on hurrying.

His first book told people to start with a one and a half mile run for time (or a 12-minute run for distance). It was meant as a test, not as an all-out competitive effort. But it brought out the latent competitor in many beginners, and it hurt some of them.

In *The New Aerobics,* Cooper deemphasizes the time test. But he still rewards rather short, fast runs. He tells in that book of measuring the fitness of two men the same age and size. Both had been running two miles a day, five days a week. Cooper found one of the men to be in "excellent" condition, while the other was barely passing. The difference was that the man in excellent shape averaged 6:45-7:00 a mile, while the other ran 10 minutes or slower.

Cooper writes, "You achieve a greater training effect if you put more effort into your exercise. Consequently, the (*Aerobics*) point system was developed so that I knew exactly how much effort was being expended. For example, if you run a mile in 11:30, you can earn three points. Run the mile in 8:30 and you earn four points."

Earn 30-50 points a week and you'll be passably fit, Cooper has found during extensive testing. The faster you go, the fewer miles you need to get those points. I can't argue with the logic of this. But I can argue with the wisdom of limiting the daily runs to 1-2 miles, and always pushing the pace.

This is what happens, and doesn't happen. With this kind of running, you're always under pressure — both physically and psychologically. You're always racing with a watch, always chasing a deadline.

Yet you never get warmed up completely in a distance this short. It takes most people 10-15 minutes to get up a good sweat and to establish a rhythm. And by that time, the one and a half to two-mile run is nearly finished. You never reach the point of "euphoria" which psychiatrist Thaddeus Kostrubala describes. He says it doesn't come until about 40 minutes, and for the first 20 minutes you feel "uncomfortable and depressed."

Also, you never get to see anything more than a small measured circuit — and you don't even see much of that when you're concentrating on the race. A slower pace lets you cover more ground, to see where you're going and think about things other than running.

And if you're keeping score, you can never go beyond 10-15 aerobic points in a single run. You can only improve your time so much before hitting your speed limit. Run a world-record two-mile, and it's still only worth 15 points. But by forgetting speed and going long, you can get as many points and more, no matter how slow you go.

I, for instance, can coast through a 30-minute run on my "rest" days and pick up 15 points. A typical day's leisurely hour is worth twice that much. I can double Cooper's weekly minimum of 30 points in a single weekend run of two hours.

I don't count points, but I know this kind of running adds up to a much more healthy and satisfying time than you'll ever find in 10-15 frantic minutes.

If Kenneth Cooper, one of running's best friends, unconsciously puts runners into a time bind, one of its severest critics unwittingly points the way out.

Dr. Meyer Friedman is a San Francisco cardiologist and co-author (with Dr. Ray Rosenman) of the best-selling book *Type A Behavior and the Heart.* In the book, Friedman labels jogging as a form of "mass murder." He writes, "First on our blacklist (of exercises) is jogging. This miserable post-collegiate athletic travesty has already killed at least scores, possibly hundreds of Americans."

The doctor sees nothing but danger in it — the risk of physical breakdown without any aesthetic compensation. He goes on, "Jogging is a form of exercise in which man transforms himself into a machine. Chug-chug-chugging along, looking neither right nor left, panting, the man-machine chugs along. And what is 'its' goal? To see if 'it' can chug-chug faster today than yesterday. And what is 'its' only joy? The soothing, miraculous feeling of relief when the chug-chugging is finished."

This is the view of a man who has never run and who has only seen the damage done by running. He judges running in the same way we would judge medicine if we only heard the malpractice cases. Friedman can't be expected to know of the far more common running experience which another cardiologist-writer, Dr. George Sheehan, describes.

"If (the critic) sees only boredom on the faces of joggers he observes, it is because he views the harried look of the average urban dweller as normal. What the jogger's face shows is not boredom but contemplation, which Thomas Aquinas described as man's highest activity save one—contemplation plus putting the fruits of that contemplation into action."

We can't expect a non-runner to understand this, so we can't ever count on Meyer Friedman's endorsement of running. But in principle, he already approves. Let me use his own words to show what I mean.

Friedman and Rosenman divide people into two distinct groups according to how they act. "Type A's" are the hard drivers; "Type B's" are the cruisers. It's the "A's" who

Friedman is concerned with, since he thinks their behavior is driving them to an early end and making life miserable for them as they hurry through it.

He writes, "It (Type A behavior) is a particular complex of personality traits, including excessive competitive drive, aggressiveness, impatience and a harrying sense of time urgency. Individuals displaying this pattern seem to be engaged in chronic, ceaseless and often fruitless struggle—with themselves, with others, with circumstances, with time, sometimes with life itself . . ."

Of these traits, "hurry sickness" and the urge to race are the most prominent. Friedman continues, "In an attempt to save time, the Type A man often creates deadlines for himself. . . . Since he very often has created not one but as many as a dozen such deadlines, he is subject to a more or less continuous time pressure. This voluntary tyranny frequently forms the very essence of Type A behavior pattern."

Running is so filled with Type A people that I almost think this kind of personality is a requirement for entering the activity-sport. The attraction is that it is quick, measurable and competitive.

Running is an efficient exercise — the most efficient, according to Kenneth Cooper. Nothing else gives so much in so little time. No time is wasted in huddles and time-outs. It's non-stop action with a self-set start and finish which don't need to be more than a few minutes apart. Impatient Type A's love this.

They are number-oriented, too, so the mathematical perfection of running is appealing. No vague, arbitrary scores here. We're dealing with basic units of time and distance — minutes and miles, and combinations of the two. How far we've come and at what speed—"progress," in other words—are easily checked and charted. In a world where so little is absolute, there's comfortable certainty in these numbers.

Type A's are highly competitive people, but competition is not fun unless you can win more often than you lose. Running lets you be a winner every day — at least to imagine you are a winner — because it requires you to race only yourself and the time-distance standards you set. You can win without having to beat anyone. You can lose only by beating yourself.

Meyer Friedman writes, "If ever one exercise was custom-made for the Type A person, jogging is the exercise." I agree with him. Running is the perfect activity for a Type A. But not in the way he means.

It has the potential to do harm, of course. I once watched a 46-year-old man die at my feet after he'd raced a half-mile, mile and six miles one after another. His diseased heart couldn't take it.

Running has the potential to exaggerate Type A actions. Every morning, I see gray-faced men, heads held at grotesque angles, breath coming in pained gasps, struggling after precious seconds. I wave and say "hi," and they won't or can't answer.

But running is what we make of it. If it can aggravate Type A behavior, it can also be a healthy safety valve for it. It can channel and drain away harmlessly the excess energy, drive, anxiety and hostility of people who otherwise would have no outlet for it.

Running can be either the cause or the cure, depending on how it's done. Faster and faster running for short distances can exaggerate Type A tendencies, while longer and more leisurely runs can bring out the Type B in you.

His ideal is a person who "is rarely harried by desire to obtain a wildly increasing number of things or participate in an endlessly growing series of events in an ever-decreasing amount of time."

Type B's aren't shiftless, slovenly men. Don't mistake their deliberate actions for a lack of direction and drive. They are "tortoises" in a "hare" world, and if you remember the story of the tortoise and the hare you know which sort of pace won the race.

Meyer Friedman writes, "Many Type B men have drive — loads of it. But they monitor it with a calendar, not a stopwatch." They pace themselves for the long haul.

The doctor is not anti-exercise. He's only against hard-paced exercise — which means he and I aren't far apart in our thinking at all.

Friedman tells in his book of a relaxed man named Ralph who walks "at least 40 minutes a day. He takes pride in the fact that he never uses an elevator to ascend a single floor in any building. He also prefers to park his car several blocks or more from any place he wishes to go, in order to get the exercise of walking."

The doctor who speaks so strongly against jogging has high praise for the long walk. He says, "Certainly, at least one hour a day and preferably more time should be spent in moving your legs and arms."

He recommends an hour on foot a day. So do I.

He recommends "moderate" physical activity which "does not cause panting, excessive acceleration of your heartbeat (that is, above 120 beats per minute) or leave you unduly fatigued."

I echo the words of Dr. Ernst van Aaken, who in turn agrees almost word for word with Friedman. Van Aaken, Europe's leading running-for-health advocate, says, "Run playfully in a state of respiratory balance (with the pulse rate rarely going over 130). There must always be — even after hours of training — the desire for joy in running faster and the ability to do so."

Friedman says, "Exercise gently at anything which gives you pleasure. . . . And always remember that it is your mind and your entire body, not necessarily your heart that are getting the benefits of exercise."

I say that you can do all of this with gentle running — running at a pace that lets you forget where the next step and breath are coming from, and instead lets you think and see and talk.

Running doesn't magically change one's basic personality. I'm not suggesting that it does, or even that such a change is desirable. By tampering with the way you are, you may wind up more frustrated than if you left your bad habits alone.

All that running can promise is to defuse some of the worst features of an explosive personality — mainly by releasing and channeling pent-up energy, draining hostility away and opening up the time to be creative.

8. Breaking

Jobs have a terrible hunger for time. They'll take all you're willing to give and still will want more. The jobs people think are important, the ones they're committed to are the worst for this.

Doctors, executives, writers. These workers fall into time traps. It's not the hourly laborers who are working only for a paycheck and who leave the job at the office or plant when they punch out at five o'clock. The professionals are the workaholics who can't find enough hours to satisfy this hunger.

Dr. George Sheehan's father was a doctor, too. He warned his boy when George was in medical school that "medicine is a jealous mistress. If not fought, medicine and your patients will devour you. You will work 80 hours a week, and the profession will always demand more. It is insatiable."

Before you know what happened, you're down to two activities: working and sleeping. You're eating while you work, and when you sleep you dream about the work still to be done. You may enjoy this, but your family and your body don't.

A friend named Jim is an executive moving up in the chain of command of a large corporation. I was running with him the other week, and he said, "I like my job, and I'm serious about it. I work hard, but not as hard as I used to."

He said he'd gotten into the habit of working overtime. There would be a special rush-rush project to get done, and he'd come in early, gobble lunch at his desk, then work till seven or eight or later at night on it. When he finished that project, there'd always be another, and another.

"My bosses were not dummies," he said. "They saw I was willing to do extra work, and they were willing to give it to me. They saw it as a reward, and I saw it as an honor."

Jim's wife and two children didn't think so much of it, though. When they saw their husband and father at all, he was exhausted, preoccupied and grumpy.

Jim's wife finally said, "The children and I are going on a vacation. I feel like a widow and they feel like orphans living this way. We're going to my parents' for a while. Call us when things are back to normal."

For two weeks, he didn't have time to call. Then Jim started thinking, "What am I doing? I'm getting ahead at work, sure, but I'm falling behind everywhere else. I'm losing my family. I'm nervous, tired and irritable all the time. I don't do anything but work."

He called his wife and said, "Come on home. There are going to be some changes made. Even if it means I don't get any more promotions, I'm not going on like this."

The first change he made was to take his full hour at lunch time. "It was hard at first. I'd have all this work piled up, and I'd feel guilty about leaving it in the middle of the day. But I left.

"I was working in Chicago then, and there happened to be a 'Y' near the office. I was out of shape, but I used to be a pretty fair athlete. I thought I'd be better off blowing off steam with a workout than going out for a businessman's lunch."

So he made a habit of going across the street to play basketball or handball at noon. Some days, though, the courts were full or he couldn't find a game. Then he'd take a little run around the track. The little run grew in length, and Jim found he liked it better than the games.

"I found out what it was like," he said, "to be wide awake at work all afternoon."

Something else happened which surprised him. "I found this wasn't an hour wasted but an hour invested. I was enough more efficient from the exercise to make up for the time out of the office."

Jim also "forced myself" not to go to work too early or come home too late. "For a while," he said, "I couldn't get rid of the feeling that I was cheating my bosses. I was so used to working the extra time that when I only put in eight hours I felt like I was working part-time. It was hard leaving work undone at night and not rushing in at six o'clock in the morning to get at it."

A funny thing happened here, too. "I found I was getting more done in eight hours than I had done in 10 or 12. Here's what I mean. Before I'd sort of resigned myself to the come-in-early, stay-late routine. So I did the Parkinson's thing. I stretched out the work to fill the time. I fiddled around a lot before getting down to work. I lingered around the water cooler and dragged out my phone calls.

"But then when I realized I had only eight hours to get my work done, I squeezed the dead space out of my day and worked more efficiently."

He promised himself two things and has kept the promises. "I'd make the most of my time at work, giving an honest eight hours. But when the time was up, I'd leave the work and worries behind until the next day."

The man from the next office came in to borrow a word or something. He was harried. He'd been fighting with a story for three days, and the match wasn't going well for him. His face showed it. He had crinkly little lines around his eyes from the strain. His hair was tossled, and his shirt was open to the third button.

In mid-sentence, he stopped and looked out the window. Two runners were approaching. They were stripped to the waist and had their shirts tied around themselves. They wore running shoes, but still had on their long pants. They worked in the office, too. Every noon, they ran to the grocery store for their lunch and back.

"Look at them," the harried writer said. "They go out and run at lunch time. I can't do that. I'm too busy to take the time."

He watched the runners for 10 seconds, then turned and rushed back to work. I left my pile of work, turned off the light and went outside to run. I was too busy not to take the time out.

Ninety-nine days in every hundred, I wake up with a run and follow it with writing. But this day, I skipped the run. I tried to write but wisely gave it up after a paragraph which was as halting and messy and senseless as something my two-year-old daughter would scribble on a page. I was pressing, and I can't do that when I write. I was rushing, and when I rush the writing is slower than when I imagine I have all the time in the world. I balled up the paper, hurled it against the wall and went to work.

Usually I ride a bike there. I like the bike because it won't let me hurry, even when I want to. It has a pace which I have to accept. The car, on the other hand, has a potential for speed which is begging to be used. I drove and exploited the speed. It was six in the morning and I was almost alone on the streets, racing the stoplights.

Usually I wouldn't work overtime. I've tried to stay out of that trap, because my work has a way of expanding to fill the time I spend at the office. If I started making a habit of spending 10 or 12 or 14 hours there, the workload would grow into it.

This was an unusual day. The magazine was already a day overdue at the printer. I was feeling the pressure of the precious minute, and the layout artist was feeling it, too. He looked at a picture I'd picked and said, "This won't do. The composition is dull and stereotyped, and it's too blurry. Get something else."

I snapped back, "Ask me, and I'll be more likely to do it."

"Okay, *will* you get another picture . . . please?" His voice dripped with sarcasm.

I looked for 30 minutes, feeling as if each of those minutes was a five-dollar bill which I was tearing in half and tossing in a fire.

I finally found the picture and took it to the artist.

"No good," he said, handing it back to me. "The chick is blurred."

I threw it at him, and the print skidded across the layout table and onto the floor.

"What the hell am I supposed to do then? Draw the damn picture?"

I went back to my room and slammed the door behind me. I hadn't sat down when the phone rang. I'd told the operator, "No calls or visitors this morning." She told the first caller that and he'd shouted, "He damn well better talk to me. I'm so-and-so of such-and-such organization, and this is very important business."

92

The next caller pleaded, "But I'm calling long distance from the East Coast, and I can't spend the money to call again."

Then there was a visitor who said, "I don't want to disturb him, but we're here on vacation, and I can't leave without meeting the editor of my favorite magazine. It'll only take a minute."

Another caller: "Oh, it's no problem. He's an old friend of mine."

Another visitor: "I have a new product I want to show him. It will be worth his while to see me, since there could be a lot of money in it for your company."

And on it went all morning. The first caller wanted to complain about an order which didn't arrive. The second one wanted to know how to enter the Boston Marathon. The visitor who only wanted a minute stayed a half-hour. The "old friend" was someone I'd met once, in 1963. The "new product" was a cheap imitation of an old shoe, and its designer was pitching for a free promotional article. Meanwhile, the magazine still wasn't getting done. My nerves were crawling out the top of my head and through my finger tips.

The three men from the next room came back from their noontime run. I resented them for their freedom. One of them shouted, "Wow, we were really moving! Thirty-three minutes for the big loop! We must have been going six minutes per mile."

"Yeah," another said. "It was great. When we go with Henderson, we slog around that loop in 40 or 45 minutes or even 50 minutes. Look how much faster we can get done when we push."

The third runner said, "We should set up records for all of our courses and try to break them when we go out. I've found you have to have a goal or you'll never go anywhere. You have to learn to hurt yourself or you'll never get there."

Some people need this kind of motivation. Some wouldn't do anything without this kind of carrot dangling just past the end of their nose. Running must have goals, competition, rewards or they can't do it. It has to be a test.

I found a long time ago that I'm not one of these people. My personality has built-in whips, so my problem is not getting going but stopping in time. If left unchecked, I'll work myself to death.

So I don't use running as an accelerator but as a brake. I don't run to speed up but to slow down—not to go anywhere but just to go. I use that time to break the hold time has on me.

Once, I would have felt self-conscious about changing into shorts in my office then walking through the reception room bare-legged — past salesmen in their coats and ties. No more. I don't notice their stares.

Once, it would have been beneath me to run in noontime traffic, on two of the busiest streets in town. I would have driven to a quiet park or to the country. Not now. I take my runs where I am.

Once, I would have squirmed at the thought of not having a shower. The stinging spray of hot water was said to be an essential part of the good feeling. Now I run, throw cold water on my face, dress and go back to work.

It sounds like a drab way to run — out the office door, through traffic, back to sit the afternoon in my own sweat. I'll admit this isn't my favorite scenario, but when the choice is between this and not running at all, between running here and now or continuing to take the pressure of work sitting down, the answer is clear.

A meditative sort of person might say to me, "Why bother with the running? It seems like a waste of time and energy. You can get the same relaxing effect by sitting in a quiet room with your eyes closed and chanting a mantra for 20 minutes twice a day."

This is how transcendental meditation is practiced: two quiet, mind-clearing, slowing-down periods each day. Reliable scientific testing has shown TM to be as restful as sleep and as calming as a strong tranquilizer. But I can't do it. One of two things happens when I'm sitting. Either my mind races right along at its same old pace, and in two minutes I'm moving again — or the break is such a relief that I fall asleep.

Sitting with my eyes closed and my head clear is not one of my talents. I have never been creative during the rare periods when I'm still and unoccupied. I stagnate when I sit. Thoughts not acted out are a pollutant. Movement is the catalyst which drains the dirty thoughts away and lets the good ones flow strong and clear.

"Okay," a slower-moving person than I might ask, "so why don't you walk? Walking seems like such a much more civilized activity than running."

Walking is safer than running and more practical. There isn't the jarring and pounding. You can do it in any clothes and shoes, any time of day without looking conspicuous. You can do it without working up a lather of sweat.

I've only recently rediscovered walking. On the noon hours when I don't run, I walk to loosen up my head. Most evenings, I walk around the neighborhood with my young daughter while my wife is running. I enjoy walking. But it's important to me for itself — not as a substitute for running. The two are nice in different ways.

Walking is a civilized, genteel exercise. Running is primitive. And I need it for that reason. I need to strip away the coverings of civilization and to sweat out its wastes.

Running feet beat out a rhythm that's missing from walking. And running to that beat shakes loose the accumulated debris in my head. Running doesn't create good thoughts, but it clears the way for them to break free.

Running takes me more places than I can go at a walk, and it takes me there sooner. During an hour's slow run, I can cover two to three times more ground than I can while walking. But it's far more important that the run produces a feeling of euphoria in one-half to one-third the time and at double or triple the strength. Type A's like me need this potent, fast-acting kind of medicine.

Yet at the same time we can't be rushed. We're running to escape that. It's a tricky balance to strike, but it can be done. These are my three hints for doing it:

1. *Create breathing space.* Stake out a large block of time for the run, and don't let anyone or anything nibble away at the corners of it. Decide how long your run is to be — in minutes or hours — then double it. I typically run an hour, so I allow two hours for rattling around. That way I never feel crowded. There's never any sense of urgency to the run.

2. *Run long.* By "long" I mean three or four or five miles or more, only you're not going to be counting miles. (I'll explain that in a minute.) You may be able to sprint and gasp and worry through a mile or two, but you won't finish a longer run this way. Well, okay you may get through it

once or twice, but you won't keep coming back for more — not when it's hurting this much. Your physical limits force you to go at a more relaxed (and relaxing) pace as the distances grow. Only after three miles or 20-30 minutes of running do you get warmed up, find your rhythm . . . and begin to experience this "euphoria" which long distance runners talk about so much.

3. *Run by time.* Here I am talking about time again. Time can be a Type A's curse if he fights it — if he tries to pack more and faster work into shrinking periods of time. But it can be his cure if he uses time in a different way — if he empties it of rush and refills it with an unpressured kind of effort.

Here's what I mean. Run for a period of time — a half-hour, 45 minutes, an hour — not by distance. When you run measured distances, the natural urge is to get them finished as quickly as possible. But an hour is an hour is an hour. Hurrying doesn't make it go any faster.

In fact, the harder you push, the longer the hour seems to take. There's something psychological which stretches and compresses time. The minutes drag when you're hurting and speed along when you're running comfortably. You're impatient for the end of a tiring run but are a little disappointed to come to the end of an easier one.

When I run by time for an unknown distance, there's no urge toward speed, because there's no way to measure it. There's no profit in getting home a minute or five or 10 minutes earlier than yesterday, because I have to keep on circling the block until my time is up. Better to spread that time over the whole run than to add it on the end.

There are other benefits to running by time: I don't need to lay out and measure my routes, and am not bound to them. I can free-lance, explore, go where my feet want to take me.

The watch gives me the measurement I need, the way to keep track of what I have run, without being a competitor. It never mocks me for not keeping up with its pace, and it never accuses me of not going as fast as I did last week or last year. It measures only the quantity of the run. The quality is decided by things other than its pace.

The morning when I was an intolerant, intolerable grump, my noontime run mellowed me out. My tension brought on by deadline pressures melted harmlessly onto the road in that hour, and that afternoon I worked as if I had all the time in the world.

The demons are still there. I'm not saying running rids me of them. But it tires them out enough that they are sleeping most of the time. Or, to mix metaphors even further, the germs of "hurry sickness" are always in me. Probably I was born with them. But as long as I keep them from spreading, as long as I keep up my resistance, the disease lies dormant and I can get on with living in a rather quiet, sane, productive way.

Say "It's all in your head" if you wish. I can't think of a more important place for it to be.

9. Traveling

The east wall of my office has two thin strips of floor-to-ceiling glass — which is great if I only look above shoulder level. There I see treetops, a sky that is often blue, and on clear days the mountains in the distance. But looking down, I see a freeway exit. And closer in is a parking lot, usually with a headlight staring in from it through each of the windows.

Used to be I could look out most days and see empty spaces in the lot. But no more. The company has grown into all of them. The only parking slots are a couple of hundred feet away.

I look out this morning and see a Porsche double-parking, blocking the escape of a Pontiac and a Triumph. The Porsche gleams with a weekend shine. The driver roars the well-tuned engine and smiles at the sound before shutting it down. Then he carefully locks and checks all the doors.

The man is in his mid-30s. His $200 suit camouflages a growing paunch, and his styled hair and sideburns are cut in such a way that they de-emphasize his growing jowl line. The man, apparently a salesman with a sample case, flips his half-smoked cigarette into the shrubbery and hurries the 10 steps into the building. Can't waste time walking from the far parking lot. Time is money.

Inside, he sits waiting a half-hour to see the boss.

The salesman shows two peculiarly American traits, both of them related to his car. First, he obviously takes better care of his Porsche than himself. He keeps it polished and tuned while letting his own exterior and engine decay. And he is caught up in the "hurry up and wait" race. He parks two minutes closer to the office door so he can wait two minutes longer in the front room.

The car has done weird things to our sense of values and pace when the health of a machine gets in the way of physical fitness and when anything less than 30 miles per hour is too slow.

People used to drive cars. Now cars are driving people, taking away our power to move and see our places worth moving through on foot and looking at closely.

Several years ago, I spent some time with an American tour group in southern Germany. Most of the Americans were runners. But they were still tuned to our way of living.

Footpaths followed the swift, clear river which ran through town and climbed the steep slopes on both sides of the river. The houses were on the hillsides, and the business district was in the valley — a mile or so from most of the homes.

The Americans dashed along the trails, trying to fill the distance as fast as they could. They seldom took time to stop and look. German families out walking stepped aside to let the runners pass, then resumed their strolls, pausing often to look at wildflowers and to watch the trout in the transparent streams.

Fit young Americans ran 5-10 miles a day, but sometimes grumbled about walking the mile down the hill to eat, then back up again. The Germans, many of them in their 60s and 70s, hiked to the store pulling two-wheeled shopping carts. They had cars, but cars were a luxury. Cars were for trips to the next town and beyond, and these people rarely went where they couldn't go on foot.

The American car is a crutch, a necessity, almost a god. It gives mobility to people who don't like the places they can go on foot. It lets them go someplace else they probably won't like any better.

God Auto gives a feeling of status to people who feel invisible without steel and glass wrapped around them. It gives a sense of identity not found in the spirit or flesh.

Above all, the car gives power to people who otherwise feel powerless. The sense of control behind the wheel is almost overpowering after a day of being controlled by other forces.

Chairman Mao says all power comes from the barrel of a gun. Gerald Ford might change that to read "Americans' power comes from a push of the accelerator pedal."

I see this every noon. Little people, assembly-line workers in the neighborhood's factories, men who've been mechanized and pushed around all morning, break and run to the parking lots with the 12 o'clock whistle. It's a Le Mans-style start.

They roar and squeal out of the lots, race up and down the semi-rural back roads. For a little while, the cars responding to their commands make them feel strong again. Strong, arrogant, sometimes unconsciously sadistic.

But the world was made to be viewed at less than 10 miles per hour. Faster than that, it is a numbing blur of images — none of them staying in sight long enough to register.

Drivers moving at 20 or 40 or 60 m.p.h. have the same glazed, fixed stare as people watching television. They are spectators watching the swirl of action through a screen until it hypnotizes them.

They can't comprehend what's going on in front of them because it's all happening so fast, and they don't notice the damage they leave in their wake because they speed away so quickly.

Speed deadens the driver's senses and kills the road he drives along. He kills the air with his noise and fumes, smothers the greenery with the garbage he tosses out, crushes small animals under his wheels. He's going so fast he doesn't see the damage he leaves, so he feels no responsibility for it.

Runners and walkers, moving through at less than 10 m.p.h., see it all from the other side of the screen.

We've been playing this game with doctors for a long time — the non-running doctors, that is, who can't appreciate the subtleties of the sport and its injuries.

A runner comes into the office and says, "I'm hurting, Doc."

"Where?" asks the doctor as he looks suspiciously at the perfectly healthy person in front of him.

"Here, on my foot." And he points to a spot on a tendon no bigger than a dime.

"I see," says the doctor. "And when does it hurt?"

"Only when I run."

"Did you hurt it while you were running?"

"Yes, it got sore after I doubled my mileage in one week."

The doctor nods and smiles paternally. "Can't you see? The answer is very simple. You hurt yourself while running. It only hurts when you run. So the solution is obviously to stop running. If you must exercise, find a substitute."

Stop running? Substitute? An addicted runner can no more stop running than stop breathing. To switch him to swimming or bicycling is no more satisfactory than giving Coke or coffee to an alcoholic.

Now let's say you're on a quiet country road west of town. You're minding your own business, a thousand miles away in thought, when a station wagon roars into your consciousness — and your running space.

Next thing you know, you're in the ditch. Your left foot is going in one direction and the rest of you in another. The ankle twists and snaps. But for now you're more angry than hurt. The car is speeding away. You try to catch a license number, but it's too late.

Only then do you look at the ankle. It's already starting to discolor and swell. You brush the dirt from your hands and knees and try to stand. A pain shoots from the ankle to the brain saying, "Please, don't put on full weight."

Just then, you see a police car. The cops make half the town's money each year catching speeders along this stretch of road. You hobble to the middle of the lane and flag him to a stop.

"Officer . . ."

"Hey," he says, "what do you think you're doing standing in the middle of the road like that?"

"I'm hurt."

"Auto accident? I don't see a car."

"No . . ."

"Motorcycle? Bike?"

"No. I was running. This big station wagon . . ."

"Running? You should know better than to run out here."

"Isn't there anything I can do?" you plead, meaning to apprehend the culprit.

"Yeah," the cop says. "You can find someplace else to run. Tracks are for runners, roads are for cars. Stay where you're safe."

Anyone who learned to run the open roads knows that a track is as poor a substitute as a treadmill in a cage is for a wild squirrel.

It's bad enough having doctors and cops overreact to what we do. But it's worse when we're stopped from doing what we *might* do. A few runners have been hit and killed by cars. A few have died of heart attacks. There are risks in running. I know them as well as anyone. But I know, too, that for every death or injury it causes, running lets a thousand other people live more fully and move more freely.

Doctors and cops who don't run can't see this. The one dramatic negative blinds them to the hundreds and thousands of subtle positives.

"Running killed someone," they reason. "Therefore, running is harmful. Therefore, no one should run."

There are always more people to warn against running because of abstract dangers than to help correct the problems.

Cops by a number of different names are quick to tell us where we can't go and what we can't do.

Several years ago, the people from our office wanted to start weekly "Fun-Runs." Just informal get-togethers which gave all kinds of runners a chance to run a measured distance, for time, with a group. No sign-ups or entry fees, no results recorded. It was to be our answer to racing which has bogged down in rules and paperwork.

The first "cop" we dealt with was called an "AAU commissioner." He was cool to the idea.

"This is highly irregular," he said. "Technically, you're breaking a half-dozen AAU regulations if you run this way. If we wanted to press a point, we could declare everyone who runs there ineligible for further competition for competing in an unsanctioned event. But I don't want to be an ogre about this. I'll send you the proper forms and you simply . . ."

No forms were ever filled out.

We called the community services director at the local college for permission to use the empty track and a bathroom for an hour or so each Sunday. He said, "Absolutely not."

"Well then," we said, "how about letting us start our runs in the corner of the parking lot, and not using any of your facilities?" That was all we really wanted, anyway. We started high to make the man think he was talking us down.

"Perhaps," he said. "But you'll have to go through proper channels. Fill out a contract . . ."

We never filled out a contract. We figured we were using only public roads and parking lots, and that we were part of the "public." Car-drivers don't have to get special permission to take Sunday joy-rides, so we shouldn't need it to take Sunday joy-*runs*.

The first week of running, a man from "campus security" demanded to know, "What's going on here?"

We told him about the runs, and that we'd talked with someone higher up in the school, and everything was okay. He accepted that. As long as the blame was shifted away from him, he didn't care what we did.

That first week, we also had a visit from the county sheriff's deputy. He, too, wanted to know what was happening on his country roads. We explained that we'd be getting together for group runs every Sunday morning. He rubbed his chin and adjusted his mirror-fronted sunglasses, as if trying to decide whether we belonged there or not.

"Well," he finally said, "I guess you can go ahead. Just don't get in anyone's way. If we have any complaints about you people blocking traffic, you'll have to go someplace else to do your jogging."

After that, the cops generally drove right past our early-Sunday-morning gathering without a glance our way. But they knew where they could go and who they could see if anything went wrong.

We got the blame for every incident involving a runner, any day of the week, any time of day, within 10 miles of the campus — even though we weren't there more than an hour or two a week and didn't run a specific course more than once a month. (The routes change every Sunday.)

One Saturday morning, another group sponsored a run on one of our courses. The race had 125 runners, and they took over the road for a time before spreading out into a single file on one side.

A man in his Mercedes met the start head-on and was engulfed by the human wave. He tried to shoulder his way through, laying on the horn as he went.

A few runners took offense at this. They yelled at him. One planted his fist on the car's hood and then shook at it at the driver. Then the wave passed. It had come and gone in 20 seconds.

The driver was furious. He raced to the starting line and shouted, "Who's in charge here?" The director tried to calm him, without much luck.

"You haven't heard the last of this," the man said as he started his Mercedes to leave. "I'm calling the police. There'll be no more joggers on this road if I have anything to say about it."

The next morning, we had a visit from the sheriff's deputy. He said, "The joggers are a traffic hazard. We had warned you before."

We protested that the only serious incidents in three years of running on and around the college campus have been the fault of people who become maniacs with a wheel in their hands and an accelerator under their right foot.

"Well," the cop said with a shrug, "you don't have to run here if you think it's dangerous."

Go someplace else. People on foot, it seems, have no protection, no rights. We can't call the police and demand that drivers use another road for a half-hour a week because they're a hazard to us. Runners can, if they hug the ditch, risk their lives in traffic, but can't take one foot of a driver's space or one second of his time.

That's the way the public roads are managed. And that's why 10,000 American pedestrians a year die there.

Pedestrians are supposed to have the right of way on most streets, and drivers are supposed to make way for them. But as Dr. James Lytle wrote in *Runner's World* "(This) is strictly a legal principle and doesn't mean much when hard steel meets soft skin."

People in cars and people on foot don't co-exist very well under the best of conditions, and no one has to try very hard for a person to get killed. Unfortunately, it is always the one walking or running who does the suffering since the one driving has a weight advantage of a ton or so.

A runner with any sense at all acts paranoid. He runs as if everyone on the road is out to get him, because every driver has the potential at his fingertips. Some advice:

1. Find the roads with the least appeal to drivers—the ones where going is slow and frustrating, and the road leads from nowhere worth being to nowhere worth seeing.

2. Run down the center line if traffic allows, and be ready to shift to the right or left as a car fills a lane.

3. Look over your shoulder often to see who might be sneaking up behind.

4. Treat every blind turn as if an ambush is waiting around it. Stay far to the outside.

5. Run defensively, in other words. Think the worst of every driver, and stay far enough from him that none of his faults rub off on you.

6. Run as if you have no rights to the road. Legally, you may have some. But practically, you're defenseless out there. You survive by your agility and cunning. You have to accept the fact that no one is on your side.

There is justice. People have been driving about a million years less than they've been running. Time has proven the human foot to be a reliable means of travel. A short time has been spent proving the car to be as much a nuisance as a convenience.

One weekend morning, I was lost in thought when a car horn brought me back home. The driver had sneaked up behind me, then gunned his engine and honked his horn as he passed. He and his passengers took great pleasure at watching me jump up about three feet and sideways about six.

A rider in the back seat on my side, a boy of about 16, leaned out the window and shouted, "Get off the road, you stupid queer." (This was still in the 1960s, and runners on the roads in shorts weren't an everyday sight yet.)

I answered only with the universal gesture of contempt as the old car disappeared around the corner leaving a trail of smoke.

A half-mile later, I came around another bend and saw the same car, parked beside the road, hood up, steam hissing from the radiator. The driver and his four passengers stared at the engine. They glared at me as I ran past but said nothing.

"I may go slow," I said. "But I get there."

I have seen the future, and it starts with a traffic jam. Eight lanes of cars sit bumper to bumper on the freeway. They are all abandoned and rusting, and what once had been a high-speed super-highway now looks like an endless salvage yard.

One day, the inevitable had happened. The road had filled up. It couldn't hold any more traffic. There was a minor fender-bender accident in the southbound lane, another northbound. The traffic was packed so tight no one could get around or off at the exits.

The drivers waited a half-hour or so to be rescued. Then they realized there wasn't any way out except on foot, so they walked to work, or to the train station, or back home— whichever was closest.

By coincidence, gas supplies finally were drying up at the same time. Gasoline, if you could get it, was $5 a gallon. The rationing limit was ridiculous: five gallons per customer per week.

People didn't give up their cars voluntarily. They wouldn't any more do that than poke an eye out. They had to be forced by the direst of emergencies to rely again on their own energy.

It was rough at first. There were great adjustments to make. Some people simply couldn't get to work in the city any more and had to find lower-paying jobs nearer to home. The unusual work of walking or biking even a few miles to the office or to the store for supplies exhausted them.

The people who had been running and walking and biking for years laughed at first at the winded, sweating hordes that filled the streets — going right down the middle because there wasn't any traffic to worry about now.

As time went on, though, it got harder and harder to tell the athletes from the other people. The differences disappeared as the latent athlete in everyone began to surface.

Paunches shrunk. Worry lines around the eyes smoothed out. Color came back to faces. Eyes took on new sparkle. People walked and talked with neighbors they hadn't known in years of living next door to each other. They looked at and saw things they'd never taken time to notice in the years of living on the same street. They felt something strange in the air, something that hadn't been there as long as they could remember. It smelled clean and sounded quiet.

The trends of a half-century began to go the other way. Workers who had uprooted trees and bulldozed away the topsoil to make room for new highways now began to break up unused highways and replace them with tree-lined pedestrian paths. The big chain stores, shopping centers and drive-in restaurants shut down one by one, to be replaced by small neighborhood operations. Smaller neighborhood schools reopened, and kids walked to and from. There was an unexplained drop in the number of people treated at hospitals, for both physical and emotional problems.

It had started when we were put back on our feet. The wave of the future, it turned out, had been the way of the past.

10. Commuting

The last several generations of Americans have grown up thinking power flows from the light switch and the accelerator. For them, the winter of 1974 was the longest, coldest and darkest in memory.

Runners were hit along with everyone else by the so-called "energy crisis." With year-round daylight saving time in effect, morning running was bleaker than ever. With fuel shortages, we came back to colder houses after runs. With gas stations closed Sundays, weekend races weren't so easy to reach.

But runners were better prepared for the national belt-tightening than the sedentary majority. Runners already knew what the others were learning: that abundance and comfort aren't limitless.

Runners knew, as an everyday fact of life in this sport, that the real energy crisis has little to do with electricity and gasoline. It involves man's first-hand dealings with the elements. The rest of the people learned this for themselves as they were forced to draw on the power resources inside themselves, to do without luxuries that have become necessities, or both.

Those of us who run (and our cousins who walk and bicycle) couldn't be too smug with our advantage. When we aren't running, we sometimes have to drive cars. We depend on the economic prosperity that is threatened by fuel shortages. We like hot showers. We were swearing at inconveniences and discomforts that winter, too. But we could be happy we decided on running as a sport instead of, say, auto racing.

As runners, we knew that scarcity, not super-abundance, is the rule of man's association with the natural world. We knew we either adapt to natural laws or are stopped by them.

Running is an exercise in "not-enough": Not enough cool breeze on hot days. Not enough warm sun on cold days. Not enough oxygen on short, fast runs. Not enough glycogen on longer, slower runs. Not enough open space. Not enough time.

Yet we manage. By adapting, we manage quite well. We come to tolerate the scarcity, even to like it for the challenge it presents. There is little comfort in running, and little convenience. But the fact that we do it and like it may be a sign that some people are tiring of the air-conditioned, over-fed, over-crowded, over-rushed style of living.

Runners voluntarily give up this life-style for at least a bit of each day. Others weren't getting as much choice in the matter in early 1974. But rather than panicking at losing their wheels, they should have looked to endurance athletes as an example of people living with scarcity and thriving on it.

Our example offered hope and opportunity to the energy bind which was being talked of mostly in doomsday terms. This was a way of returning — on a personal basis, at least — to a slower, simpler, more natural and less mechanical way of living.

Pleading for people to get fit hasn't worked. Trying to scare them into it hasn't accomplished much more. Perhaps requiring them to get back on their feet — walking, running, bicycling not for sport or exercise but for transportation — will someday succeed where propaganda has failed.

Monday through Friday, Joe Viverito leaves his Long Island home for the 10-mile commute into New York City. After his work day, he reverses his route and goes home. The difference between Joe and a million other New York commuters is that he goes to work and back on foot.

Viverito works for a public relations firm which polishes the images of the oil companies. "People live by symbols," he says, "and if they see me running, perhaps they will be motivated to cooperate and find ways to save energy. Despite all the unknowns about the energy situation, the need for everyone to conserve energy will be crucial to economic stability over the next few years."

Joe already was doing 12-15 miles a day when he hit upon the to-work-and-back idea one winter. He said then, "All I'm doing is switching my running time, adding a little extra mileage and losing some sleep."

I don't have the exact figures to quote here. But a recent national survey reported that something like four in five Americans drive their own cars to work and back each day. Most of the others take public transportation. Only about one in a hundred walks.

The main streets are clogged, the sidewalks are empty. At 7:30 in the morning in winter of 1974, a runner on his way to work could smile smugly, knowing that the advantage had swung at least temporarily to him.

Lines at the gas stations were backed up a mile or more. Maybe he was imagining it, but motorists seemed to glower at him as he ran down the line.

He crossed the freeway. The morning was still dark, and a river of headlights, four lanes across in both

114

directions, ran as far to the north and south as he could see. The traffic was moving slower than he was.

True, he had been sucking up some of the auto fumes on the busier streets. And there had been some risk of being bumped. But all in all, running wasn't a bad way to get to work.

He'd put in a brisk seven miles, and his super-oxygenated brain was ready to do some heavy thinking. He sponged off, put on fresh clothes and sat down to eight hours at the desk before running back home.

By running this way, he'd solved a number of problems: getting to work during the gas shortage (the wait at gas stations was as long as two hours that winter); getting to work quickly (the bus would have taken an hour each way); and most of all, getting in extra mileage (name a more practical way to go two hours a day).

This is any runner's answer to "I don't have time to run because of work." Anyone who has time to commute has time to do some or all of it on foot.

Carl Muckler of St. Louis writes: "At least four runners I talked to have made the complete evolution from track to transportation. In this process, the novice starts by going around the block until the cat-calls get to him.

"From there, it's the closest cinder track, where running appears normal. Then a farther drive to the Tartan track. After a certain amount of boredom, it's off the track and onto the campus, where still about everything's acceptable.

"Next, with the confidence of a few club-level events, it's back to running in the neighborhood, to conserve workout time and add miles. Finally, it's to and from work, avoiding a still further waste of time (and, may I add, gasoline)."

115

Ron Hill, a talented and inventive British marathoner, says mileage in the neighborhood of 100 a week is essential for anyone with serious long distance racing intentions. But the time pinch can be severe at this level.

"For the working man, and more especially the married man," Hill says, "it is not easy to fit in around 100 miles a week without conflict to social and family life. But with careful planning, it can be done. The easiest way of accomplishing this is by training twice a day — once before breakfast and once in the evening, preferably before the evening meal."

Does this mean getting up two hours before the birds, and eating dinner at 9 p.m.? Not at all. Hill leaves home an hour before he's due at work. He gets home an hour or so after the workday ends. By commuting on foot, he logs 15-20 miles a day. And his children still know they have a father.

Almost any runner has this option available. Distance and route are the main barriers. There's no sense in running to work if the office is just around the corner. But if the distance is a couple of miles up to 8-10, you're ideally situated for commute running.

The distance is ideal, that is, if it isn't all freeway or if it isn't dotted with stoplights every 200 yards. Shorter distances are better than longer ones because they give you a chance to detour away from busy thoroughfares and to use a variety of courses.

Ron Hill runs straight to work each morning, seven miles. But on the way home, he goes a different way to total between 8-1/2 and 12. "I am not advocating that everyone should try to run seven miles in the morning," he says. "This became necessary by force of circumstances, representing the shortest route between home and work."

William Proxmire, the senator from Wisconsin, is America's best known running commuter. He lives 4-5 miles from Capitol Hill and runs at least one way most days. Proxmire has anticipated the argument of those who say, "Wait a minute. I don't live five miles from work. I work 10 (or 15 or 20 or more)."

"The answer to that is that you park on the outskirts (usually you can park there more cheaply, more easily, usually for nothing), and just get out and run the remaining two, three, four or five miles — whatever you want to run and can fit into your day."

Another argument is, "But I don't have a locker room at work. I can't do this without a shower."

Proxmire says, "I'm very lucky in that I have a locker room here in the Senate . . . (But) I used to do it just using a bathroom. I'd come in, sponge down and change into my regular clothes. That worked fairly well."

Ron Hill is more blunt: "In England, we don't shower as much as you do in America. It isn't really necessary. You're not really dirty, you know. I just sort of sponge off and dress. Besides, my AM workout isn't that fast."

John Loeschhorn, former manager of the Starting Line Sports branch of *Runner's World*, ran to work and back each day. We didn't have a shower. No problem. He sponged off at the sink and dressed for work. Several others of us did the same, and still do, even though a shower is still in the company's future.

Getting clothes to work seems to cause more trouble than foregoing the luxury of a hot shower. John strapped on a small nylon backpack. I've seen another runner carrying his clothes rolled up in each hand like oversized batons. Since I only run in to work every other day, I can carry my clothing in by bike on alternate days. None of these solutions is ideal. John lived with the bouncing pack on his back. The man on the street never has his hands free. I'm forever forgetting my belt, socks, etc.

There are problems with running to work. But the benefits outweigh these. The biggest benefit, Loeschhorn said, is consistency — two runs every day, five days every week for him. He didn't take a weekday run longer than seven miles, yet he went 90 miles or more a week. That regularity resulted in his fastest times at all long distances.

Ted Corbitt, now in his 50s, found years ago that running to work and back was the best way to get the high mileage he wanted.

Hal Higdon writes of Corbitt in On the Run from Dogs and People, "Sometimes he will rise at four in the morning and cover 30 miles . . . Even on his easy workout days, he runs to catch the subway. One morning he ran past a corner where two men stood. 'Man,' one of them said, 'that cat's late for work every morning!'"

11. Waking

In winter, my days are going downhill before the sun is up. I'm a morning person by nature. I peak early in the day and like to do my running and writing before I start winding down. But this is ridiculous. This isn't early morning. It's still night.

I stumble out into the gloom, trying to imitate a runner. Right after that, I try to write things that other people might read. By 6:30 or 7 o'clock, the part of the day I look forward to most is over. The sky is just starting to lighten at the horizon. It's time to get ready for work.

There's nothing wrong with work. I don't mean to give that impression. As jobs go, mine is as good as anyone could want. But like all jobs, it has its time and energy demands. They push the best part of my day into its darkest corner, just before dawn.

I can barely move until the cloud of sleepiness lifts, and that takes a half-hour most days — half to all of a weekday run. I'm awake enough to write when I get home, but I have to hurry through it to get to work on time.

It isn't the most efficient and creative time, this first hour to hour and a half of the day. But it's all I have. After a dozen years of running and writing the first thing each morning, I've forgotten how to wake up any other way. When I miss either one, the day never really gets started.

I realize, of course, that everyone doesn't react this way. There are morning people and night people — so-called "larks" and "owls." I'm a lark, and morning running makes my day. But it might destroy the day of an owl who doesn't normally reach full flight until sundown.

I checked the responses to a training survey taken several years ago — first throwing out the students and odd-hour workers with the luxury of midday time, and then eliminating the rare birds who run morning *and* night. I wanted to see how working runners solved this problem of fitting their running into a busy day. Did they make time before or after work?

Notice I said "*make* time." Working runners aren't handed spare hours. You have to carve them off of one end of the day or the other, and guard them jealously. The time you make isn't usually the best time of day. Most often, it's the *least bad* time, at one of the dark ends of the day.

Of more than a thousand runners questioned, 38 percent said they preferred getting out early; 59 percent chose to wait until evening. The other 3 percent ran during the lunch break at noon.

Night people outnumber morning people among runners. Physically, people in general operate best in the P.M. Studies at an Irish medical college have shown "maximum performance for 30 athletes occurred between 5 P.M. and 7 P.M. All six runners tested did better in the evening than in the morning between 7 A.M. and 8 A.M."

This doesn't surprise any runner who compares morning and evening times. I often run to and from work. My 6 A.M. times are almost invariably as much as a minute per mile slower than the 5 P.M. times — and at equal effort.

But I've also read someplace, I can't remember where right now, that there's a significantly higher dropout rate among people who exercise in the evening. It's easy to guess why. About the only thing standing in the way of a morning run is sleep. At night, there's working late at the office, dinner to hold, unbreakable engagements, TV to watch — any number of reasons to skip a run here, another there, until you're missing more than you're making.

The noon hour is an ideal time for those who can spare it. Only a few people run then. But judging by what's happening locally, this is a growing group. I know of runners meeting at five different sites. As many as 100 take off from the Stanford University track each weekday at 12 o'clock.

The noontime runners list the advantages: daylight, relatively warm weather, group support, a healthy alternative to businessman lunches. One man says, "I couldn't stay awake in the afternoon without my run. It's the only chance I have to break away from my desk."

But I can't or won't wait that long. I've learned to live with the limitations of the predawn by seeing that each negative feature has a benefit to go with it.

Sure, it's hardest to get up and out at that hour. But it's easiest then to make time for a run.

Sure, it's dark. But it would be at night, too. And morning darkness is less depressing to me than evening darkness. The day is promising to come alive before work. Afterwards, it's dying.

Sure, it's cold. But it's also cleaner and quieter than at any other time of day. The pollution level has dropped overnight. No one is wide awake enough to heckle. Even the dogs are still asleep.

Sure, you're stiff and sore. But your early-warning system against injuries is the most sensitive now. Pay attention.

Every little pain is multiplied by a factor of about five after a night's sleep. Runners who've run a marathon on

Sunday barely can hobble to the bathroom on Monday morning. When I was going through a siege of heel trouble several years ago, I couldn't get my foot down flat on the floor for the first five minutes out of bed.

A doctor asked, "What time of day do you run?"

I said, "First thing."

He said, "Maybe you should wait until afternoon. You're aggravating your problem by running stiff."

His advice went unheeded.

Another doctor told me later that I was chronically stiff and should do corrective stretching exercises. I listened this time. He said, "Do them before and after running." After was no problem. But before . . . no way!

My flexibility, which is up to minimum standards after years of stretching, is less than half of normal in the early morning. I can barely tie my shoes.

There's some risk of injury in running stiff like this. *Runner's World* publisher Bob Anderson, more of an "owl" and a faster trainer than I am, says, "If I run in the morning for any length of time, I always end up getting hurt."

I don't think I can directly blame any of my problems on running then, but I certainly am limited in the places and paces available.

Down at the end of my street is a large schoolyard with a dirt path around the outside — a great place for soft-ground running. I can use it only six months of the year, though, because I can't trust ground I can't see. The street-lighted roads have to do.

Running isn't as efficient at this hour. To be safe, it has to be slow — at least in the early miles. Tight muscles rebel against speed the way a cold car sputters and dies if it's goosed too soon. I have to ease into my runs, barely exceeding a walk for the first 10 minutes or so.

The benefit of, say, eight miles at 8-1/2-minute pace may not be as great as the same distance a minute per mile faster — which I might have in the afternoon for the same effort. But I can't wait all day.

I can wait a little, though. Even a half-hour means a lot. On Saturdays, when I get up and drive to the country for a long run, I feel much looser for the delay.

A while back, I tried writing first and then running on weekdays to get the same benefit. The running was fine. But writing before the sleep was out of my head resulted in an incredible bunch of gibberish which no one will ever see.

More recently, I've taken to shaving and showering *before* I run. It sounds weird, I know. But it works. It wakes me and loosens me up, and the shower does enough cleaning to last on 35-degree days. The run is smoother for it, the writing is more intelligible, and I still get to work on time.

Yet I miss the daylight and envy runners who don't have to hurry around so early. John A. Kelley, for instance, is retired now. The two-time Boston Marathon winner says, "Personally, I am an early riser, and I protect my own program as an after-breakfast thing. Generally, I'm up at 6 o'clock for a light breakfast. Then I sit around reading the morning paper for an hour. By 7 o'clock, it's light enough and my 66-year-old body is ready for a workout."

That's a civilized way to start any day.

12. Seeing

Down at the end of a street where we once lived, not 200 yards from the front door, was an apricot orchard. The orchard was 13 acres. It had 20 rows of trees, 20 trees to a row, lined up like soldiers at morning inspection.

The orchard was surrounded by the city: an overly manicured park to the north, condominiums to the east and south (we lived to the south) and apartments to the west. The orchard had been many times bigger before the land had become too valuable for fruit trees.

The orchard was criss-crossed with paths, light-colored, hard tracks in the dirt left by trucks of pickers, and by kids short-cutting to school. I liked to run along those paths. The surface was good for the legs, and running among the trees let me imagine for a while that there wasn't a city all around. I went to the orchard a couple of times a week and hoped I could keep doing it as long as I lived nearby. It was too much to hope.

The local school district owned the land and leased it out to farmers. Then the school officials became hard up for money. They put the land up for sale. The farmers of course couldn't afford it. They'd be pushed off of some more growing land, which had been their story in this valley for the last 30 years.

Developers wanted the orchard and could pay top dollar for it (a sum they'd get back many times over when housing went up). But first the school offered the land to the city on the condition that it would be protected as permanent open space. The city had to take this to the voters in the form of a bond issue. The question, in simplest terms, was, "Will you pay thousands of dollars for this land which forever will sit idle?"

Such extravagance couldn't be tolerated in hard times. Voters couldn't pay that kind of money to keep up a working place for a few dusty, brown-skinned farmers, a nesting place for a flock of noisy crows, a toilet for pampered house dogs and a running place for sore-legged people. The bond issue failed.

The night after the election, the local paper reported that developers were lining up at the school district offices that morning, checkbooks in hand.

A few weeks later, one of them rolled his bulldozers into the orchard at the end of our street, and by noon had flattened and trucked away the trees. A fence went up around the bare ground and building began.

In fairness, I have to say that I'd been on the other end of this fight to keep space open. A year earlier, the land we lived on had been part of the orchard. The people who built our condominium had cleared away the trees and built on the land.

The people living in the houses to the west of us didn't like this. They went screaming to the city planners. "Stop the development!" they protested.

They won some concessions. A fence went up between the houses and the new development. But the building went ahead as planned. The people to the west stayed angry. An arsonist burned one of the almost-finished units. The fire-bomber was never caught, but the suspicion was that he lived close by.

The neighbors eventually settled down to glaring at us... as their own neighbors had when their houses had taken over an orchard... and theirs before them. And so on all over town as housing sprouted and open space shrank.

It's okay for me to take my space. But you can't have what's left.

Leevi Seppanen, a visiting Finn, had lived all of his life within sight of the Soviet frontier. And George Chen had come to the United States from Hong Kong after growing up within sight of the Chinese border. We were running together on a winter Saturday morning.

I like to free-lance when I run — explore new trails instead of sticking with the familiar ones. It drives crazy the people who have to know just how far and fast they've gone. I hit lots of dead-ends this way, but also sometimes discover new paths which lead to places the main routes couldn't have taken us.

This day I said, "I've been looking at the horse trail there for a couple of years. Want to see where it leads?"

Leevi and George nodded. We hopped the low barbed-wire fence with the "Keep Out!" sign. I motioned at it with my head. "That's for people with motorcycles and guns — people who can cause damage. No one here cares about us runners."

The path led downhill into dense woods beside a creek. The creek was running bank-full with the winter rain from higher in the foothills. It cut the path in two and was too wide and muddy to cross without the run turning into a swim.

No problem. A water department dirt road paralleled the creek on our side. We followed it, but it ran out beside a holding tank after less than half a mile.

126

We looked up above and saw a clearing. "This way?" I asked, pointing up.

The others were starting to doubt my sense of direction but didn't know a better way out. So they said, "Sure, whatever you want."

We scrambled and half-crawled up the hill through wet underbrush. Then at the top, sure enough, there was a road a few hundred yards away. A beautiful road it was, too. A narrow, gray one cutting through a green field. As far as we could see in either direction along the road, there were no buildings or cars.

"How could we have missed a running place like this all these years?" I wondered.

We sloshed across the marshy field, sinking to our ankles in the muck, to reach the road. Then it was as if we'd been picked up on radar. We hadn't been on the road more than 50 steps when an olive green pickup rushed at us.

There wasn't any doubt it was meant to intercept us. "What should we do?" George Chen asked.

I'd thought before about what to do when challenged for trespassing. "One of three things," I said. "One, pretend we are deaf. Answer the man in sign language. Two, pretend we are near-sighted, and that we left our glasses at home and didn't see any signs. Or three, pretend we can't speak any English. Leevi, you answer him in Finnish. George, you say something in Chinese. I'll keep quiet."

The man was out of his pickup before it was completely stopped. "Okay," he shouted, "that's as far as you go. Stop in your tracks."

We stopped, with eyes and mouths wide open. The man looked like a soldier who'd strayed from his unit and didn't know World War II had ended 30 years earlier. He was dressed in all-green and wore a hard-hat and high boots. He gripped a rifle across his chest like a sentry on guard duty.

I stammered, "We... we didn't mean any harm... just got lost." Then we beat it in the other direction. I've never known where that road leads or why the guard was so threatening, and never mean to find out.

Once we reached the relative safety of the highway, Leevi the Finn said, "I've lived by the Russian border all my life. I've run wherever I pleased and nothing like this has ever happened."

Space and time are the runner's luxuries. There never seems to be enough of either one when you live on a crowded schedule and in a crowded suburb. To keep your sanity at times and places like this, you have to take movement when and where you can find it. Here, it may mean exploring the city dump early in the morning or at lunch time.

The dump and the city sewage treatment plant are in the Baylands. This is the mudflats and fill land between the freeway and the San Francisco Bay itself. People here generally consider this the slums and won't even drive down to this part of town.

Our office complex is on the fringe of this area, next to the freeway. The city doesn't bother to maintain the few streets to the east of us. The bottom has long since dropped out of the asphalt roadways, and there are no sidewalks or streetlights here.

A few hundred people live in the Baylands, most of them poor. They are a mix of aging Italians, newly arrived Mexicans and remnants of the 1960s hippie movement.

This is the closest thing our town has to "country." The people of the Baylands look like real farmers, not like the ones on the estates in the hills who play at farming. The small plots surrounding the houses of the Baylands are cluttered with falling-down fences, littered with junk machinery, and scruffy with weeds that need mowing and trees that need trimming. Chickens peck on the front lawns. Beef and dairy cattle graze in a pen in back.

The use of the land gets more basic the farther out you go in the Baylands. Land is precious here, because it wasn't always here. Once this was only mud and water. It was reclaimed from the Bay years ago, and someday it will be part of the Bay again. The fill land rides on an unstable bed of mud. When the big quake comes — it's not a question of *if*, only *when* — the land will go glub, glub, glub as it slowly sinks from sight. This is another reason not many people live here. Those who do are living several miles from the shore of the Bay.

Where the housing leaves off, truck farms begin — acres and acres of onions and beets and broccoli. This gardening is fairly mechanized. One man and a tractor can handle the plowing and irrigating. But at planting and picking time, the work is basic again. Dozens of stoop-laborers move slowly up and down the rows.

Out near the Bay at sowing and reaping time, there isn't anything motorized in sight. The pace is 50 miles per hour slower than on the Bayshore Freeway just a few miles away. The hurried, harried people on the freeway don't know this contrast exists so close to them, and don't have time to find out.

The last and best area is the most basic one of all. Unless you work for the electrical, water or sanitation department and have a key to the gates, you can't drive there. Hardly anyone has a key or a reason to go.

Miles of levees have been reclaimed from the mud. The paths along the levees are dirt and not more than a car-track wide. There aren't any trees this far out, and nothing grows except swamp grasses. The only development out here is the city dump and sewage treatment plant, but these are hidden from view on all sides.

The levees, mudflats and tidal pools belong to the birds. The only sound is their screeching and the constant low moan of the wind off the bay. There's a desolate beauty to this scene.

I start at the office and go back in time, back first to the farms I used to know, to the fields and finally to the Bayshore as it has always been except for the levees which let me intrude here on foot.

In five minutes, I run from overcivilized to primitive. I start with the Bayshore Freeway rumbling at my back. I start from an ultra-modern, air-cooled office. A few hundred yards later, I turn off the pavement onto dirt. The going is soft from then on. The air is increasingly quiet.

The traffic noise disappears behind me as I turn onto the nearest levee. Someone has made a hole in the fence here. To the left is a Christmas tree farm, to the right an onion field. The combined smells of pine, onions and salt blown in from the bay fill my nose.

Farther along is a six-foot chainlink fence. On it is a black and white sign: "No trespassing—Hazardous Area." A runner looking for good places to go can't let a sign like that stop him, since the best places are always fenced off and posted.

It takes a runner to get in. There isn't more than six inches of space between the gates. I squeeze through, into the true Baylands. I know no one will bother me here. In all the time I've run the levees, I've never met another person or seen a vehicle.

The Baylands are under the approach to San Francisco Airport. I've flown in here many times. And from even a few hundred feet up, the land below looks dead — brown and lifeless. Brown grass, brown mud, brown water. Only at ground level have I been able to see that this is one of the liveliest places I travel. The wildlife blends in so well with the scene that I can only see it when I'm traveling the same ground.

A startled brown jackrabbit looks at me. He's paralyzed for a moment. Then he flicks his long ears and dashes down the trail ahead of me, making zig-zag evasive maneuvers as he goes.

A short-legged brown ground squirrel lies sunning himself. He sees me and slides quickly into a hole, as if pulled in by a string.

A brown mama duck waddles across the trail towing four little ones. She scolds them for not moving fast enough and scolds me for making them move.

The brazen gulls barely notice me. They move out of the way reluctantly and briefly to let me pass, but quickly take back their old places.

A great bird sits on a fence post. He's three feet tall, most of this neck and legs. His head turns slowly as I run past, but he doesn't bother to move. The birds know they belong here and I'm just passing through.

Now I read that the city wants to make a park of this entire Baylands area — a park with roads attracting 10,000 cars a day.

13. Meditating

Once each day, at about the same time and for about the same amount of time each day, I quietly go out of my mind. I leave my rational mind behind and spin out for at least a half-hour, usually longer. It's brain-washing in a positive sense — in the sense of cleaning and clearing gummed up thinking by intentionally not concentrating on any thoughts for a while.

A stock question asked by people who don't run of those who do is, "What do you think about all that time you're out there alone on the track or road?"

The best answer is "nothing."

Dr. Leonard Reich, a New York City psychologist and runner, answers his friends this way: "I tell them cryptically that I try not to think about anything. In fact, I concentrate on clearing my mind of all thoughts so as to become receptive to the activity in which I am engaged. I call this 'meditative running.'"

Of course we can't stop thinking, but we can stop guiding our thoughts in specific directions. The first step in "meditative running," Dr. Reich says, is to "focus oneself in the present, to become aware of the here and now. This means to be receptive, to open awareness to all internal and external stimuli, to allow all the forces in the immediate situation to have equal attention."

In short, let the mind float or leap at will from one subject to another, without focusing on one or giving it greater value than another.

The same principle applies to transcendental meditation — which, incidentally, Dr. William Glasser calls the second most effective path to positive addiction, behind running. Dozens of books praise TM. I quote one of them not because it is best but because it is the only one I've read.

In *Tranquility Without Pills,* Jhan Robins and David Fisher say, "The most important thing during transcendental meditation is to avoid concentrating on anything in particular. Concentrating holds the mind at one level and will not allow it to submerge into deeper levels of consciousness."

At least on the surface, sitting (TM) and moving (running) meditation seem quite similar. The TM teachers say to meditate for 20-minute periods. Psychiatrist Thaddeus Kostrubala says the same for running. TM meditators rhythmically chant a "mantra." Steady breathing and the beat of the feet set the runner's rhythm. The thought (or no-thought) processes are alike.

However, TM is wrapped in ritual and mystery, and requires a teacher and a training fee. If you don't learn to meditate properly, you don't reach the "transcendent" mental state. Running, on the other hand, is simple and free. People who thought of it as meditation are meditating with it every day. The out-of-your-mind state is easy to reach — when a few basic conditions are met.

The conditions for "meditative" running are almost identical to the ones Dr. William Glasser listed for "addictive" running in Chapter Two.

1. *Run alone.* You can't have anyone else intruding on your non-thoughts.

2. *Simplify.* Run over an uncomplicated route and by an uncomplicated routine which don't demand constant attention.

3. *Go gently.* Run at a steady, non-exhausting pace. If you're too tired, all you can think about is how much you hurt and how far it is to the finish.

4. *Race not, judge not.* The mind can't float if it is fretting about the other runners ahead or behind, or about the hands of a clock rushing onward.

5. *Allow time* — a half-hour to an hour a day. It takes much of that time to clear away the worst of the garbage.

6. *Spin free.* If you catch yourself clinging to one idea for too long, submerge it back into the unconscious.

"I have talked with many physically addicted people, runners and others," writes Dr. Glasser in his book *Positive Addiction*, "and it is this state of mind that almost all of them describe — a trance-like, transcendental mental state that accompanies the addictive exercise."

"Transcendental" is a rather large and pompous word to describe the result of what is essentially a mind-clearing and cleaning process. You are a garbage man working in your own head.

The brain is a garbage bin which collects sensory stimuli at an astounding rate. It takes just about everything it's offered in the way of sights, sounds and smells. Usually we're so busy taking things in that we don't have time to process them.

Running at a "meditative" pace gives us a chance to catch up. We can stand aside and watch ideas float past as if they're pieces of garbage on a conveyor belt. We can poke casually through the information, plucking out the few bits worth saving and letting the waste fall away. The recycled pieces are automatically stored for later use.

Martha Klopfer is a Quaker, accustomed by years of training to quiet contemplation. The North Carolina woman is also a long distance runner who spends an hour or more each day on the road. This combination solves a lot of problems for her.

She told Dr. Glasser in *Positive Addiction*, "Sometimes problems get solved while I am running, or I think of things to say to people. But it is not a 'figuring-out' process — more of a sudden flash of insight that comes when you are least trying to find an answer. I think worrying and running are impossible to do at the same time."

A way to handle a thorny problem, then, is not to worry about it but to run away from it — literally. When I'm worried, which is fairly often, I go through the following process:

1. Define the problem.

2. Think a little bit about the alternatives it poses.

3. Forget it. Send it diving into the unconscious.

4. Go running and think about nothing in particular.

5. Wait for an answer to come bubbling unexpectedly to the surface. Nine times in 10, it will come up.

After meditating comes creating, which is putting meditation into action. I write right after I run because more good ideas come to me when I'm running and not thinking about writing than when I'm staring at a blank page, straining to draw out the right words.

I'm not saying running will turn you into a creative genius. It won't magically put talent into your head and fingers. But it will clear away the accumulated debris which clogs up what is there.

14. Creating

I'm a writer by trade. Not a great writer. I'll never turn out a best-seller or a classic because the people who do that are artists. I'm more of a journeyman. Writing isn't a gift I was born with. It's something I learned with practice over the last 15 or so years and am still learning. I've learned it well enough to earn a living this way, but that's about all.

I'm a runner by habit. Not a great runner. I'll never win anything or run any times worth printing. The hares do that, and I'm more of a tortoise. I'm not a gifted runner, but running is something I've learned over 20 years and am still learning. I now know how to run well enough to stay reasonably fit and happy with it.

After so many years, I need both writing and running. I need to write to keep eating, and to run to keep sane and healthy. To get what writing and running offer, I have to do both of them each day, day after day, as far into the future as I can see.

If these two are to keep doing what they're supposed to, I have to keep up with them. That's the important goal: not to stop. Keep moving and knock down anything that gets in the way of free movement.

Starting is the hardest part of any movement. The biggest obstacle is fear — fear of the first word or the first step. I've had lots of time in 20 years to look at that fear, to see why it develops and what can be done to put it down. I've learned from running how to deal with it in my writing and from writing what to do in running. The two are a lot alike.

The ailment any writer fears most is "writer's block," a constipation of words. The best description of it I've heard is it's "like a five-pound chicken trying to lay a 10-pound egg." It's part how-can-I-say-this-well, part nothing-to-say and part too-much-to-say-but-can't-say-it-right.

I had a day like this recently. I had a page to write, only 300-400 words, normally a quick 15-20 minutes' work. I had notes in front of me and ideas in my head, but they wouldn't jump to the paper. The more I prodded them, the more they balked. My wads of false-starts piled up in the corner where I threw them. My brain tightened up as much as my fist, which was breaking the pen. I couldn't scribble out an intelligible sentence.

It took me an hour and a half to write that page, and it wasn't even a good page. It didn't flow. It plodded. I'd forgotten the basic lesson: I can't do things perfectly on first try and can't draw words from an empty pool. It's like trying to put all-out racing before gentle training.

Most of my writing "training" is stream-of-consciousness-type stuff. It isn't worth reading at this stage, and may never be. This is okay. If nothing else, this writing is good psychotherapy. If polished words come out, it's only by accident. I'm writing for quantity, not quality. I want to get the thoughts down as fast as they bubble up from the source, and get as many of them into the loose-leaf binder as possible.

It's important at the start not to dam up the stream of consciousness. Let it flow, swift and clear, to a holding pool. The finished stories will come from this pool. The deeper it is, the better the stories will be.

The same is true with running. As long as the daily flow remains steady and strong, the pool of fitness will be adequate for rare all-out bursts. In other words, take care of the first steps and the final ones will take care of themselves.

There is always some reluctance to make that first scratch on a clean sheet of paper or to stick the first leg out the front door. I still have to wrestle with myself just a little to shift from thinking to writing, from rest to motion. It takes the same discipline to do this as it does to plunge into cold water. There's an initial shock, but it's refreshing later.

My trick, when I write as when I run, is not to look past the first few words or few hundred yards. Expect the first steps to be slow and jerky. It takes some time to get going. Don't force the direction or pace. Let the writing and running find their own course. Let them pick up their own flow.

I've had "running blocks" when I forgot to run this way. My first year of college, I got so scared of not running far or fast enough that I couldn't run at all. My times for the mile fell off by half a minute as I tied up from fright. When the season ended, I quit completely.

I started again, but made some more mistakes. One was timing myself every day — running measured courses against the clock and keeping records of the times. It was okay at first, when I could break records without trying. But as times went down, effort and tension went up. I had to break a record every day, so every day's run was a race.

At the same time, I was counting miles. Each week, I had to run more miles than the week before. This too was no problem at first — until I climbed past 50 and 55 and 60 miles.

This combination of escalating pace and distance finally left me too sore, tense and frustrated to be anything but relieved when a run ended. I had to find something more relaxed if I was to go on.

I quit timing myself and quit counting miles. I hit on a pace I could hold indefinitely, and a kind of running I looked forward to every morning. I tried to pick out some lessons for keeping me running and to apply other places where I might get dammed up.

1. *Start without an end in sight.* No matter how crappy you feel, short of being in a cast or in bed with a 102-degree fever, start the run. Reserve judgment on how it's going to go until you are 5-10 easy minutes along. It takes that long to pick up the flow, and you'll know by then if you're going to pick it up that day. If you still feel like you're running upstream, don't fight it. Stop and hope for a better tomorrow.

2. *Remember that anything is better than nothing.* Too much is made of quantity and quality. One doctor says, as I have hinted, you must do six miles or more. Another tells you to stay at 1-1/2 miles, but to push down the pace. Both are probably right from their own points of view, but they unwittingly scare some people away from running with these formulas — people who can't go 1-1/2 miles in 12 minutes and can't go six miles without wheels under them. Even a trickle of running adds something to the pool of fitness.

3. *Let the pace find itself.* No stopwatch can tell how you feel or how fast you should be running. The best pace is one that tiptoes along the edge between comfort and discomfort. You can't plan it because it changes from day to day, even from mile to mile within a run. The best pace is the one that trains but doesn't strain you. No one can tell you the difference. It's something you feel.

4. *Run for yourself.* Don't be intimidated by other people's standards, what they have done and are doing, what they expect of you and what you in turn expect of yourself. Learn to judge realistically your own present limits.

5. *Run for today.* Ron Clarke, a world record setter a dozen times over, once said that a runner is never so depressed as in the few days after a record race. It's then that he asks himself, "How do I top this?" Accept the fact that every run can't be a record. Learn to take pleasure in less than your best.

That's what training is: "less than your best." Ninety or more miles of every 100 have to be at less than full speed. That's the way the pool of fitness fills up. Race-type runs draw from that pool and dry it up when they come too hard, too often. A runner's first concern is keeping the stream flowing, filling the pool.

A writer works the same way. He or she can't turn out a classic every day, and must see the value in doing less. Good writing is the product of starting with the first word and putting down whatever comes out after that, at whatever rate and in whatever sequence it comes. This rough kind of stream-of-consciousness writing fills the pool

140

from which readable stories are drawn. Without the pool, these stories can't develop.

The writer's and the runner's first obligation is to keep the stream free of obstruction and pollution — to keep moving no matter what.

The best comes later. Taking the best from the writing or running pools is an editing job. It's filtering what you've done in private and deciding what is worth showing to the public in articles or races.

It isn't easy showing what you're capable of doing at your maximum. It's draining and often painful work. Exposing yourself in public is one of the hardest things you can do. Yet it's inevitable that you do it if the pool has filled to overflowing. You have to drain some of it away, to make room for more filling.

The best has to come out as long as the stream keeps flowing. The easiest work has to force out the hardest.

15. Escaping

My dad grew up in the same little Iowa town as his children did. It was so small that if two cars backed up behind each other on Main Street, the drivers called it a traffic jam. So small that everyone knew everybody else's family secrets.

Dad went away for a while to try for fame and fortune in the city. He worked at a job much like mine, as an editor of a specialty magazine. He quit when he was younger than I am now — partly because, he said, "I couldn't stand the constant pressure of deadlines."

The other part was that he couldn't stand the pressure of all those people in the city. Years later, when the family was settled back in our hometown, Dad said, "Nice people in masses become asses."

I had no idea then what he was talking about, because I never saw people in masses except a couple of times a year — at the State Fair and the Drake Relays. And those times were kind of exciting for a country boy.

Otherwise, I went for weeks at a time without ever seeing a face I didn't recognize. The small-town folks often seemed too close. They seemed to know each other too well and to smother each other with friendliness. Living there was like having a family of 300.

Then I turned 18. I was itching to leave home and family, and to try my legs in the bigger world — which soon enough showed me what my father meant about "masses of asses."

The little town was tolerant of my running. Oh, a few people there giggled behind their hands at me or made crude comments, but all in all things were okay. I'd shown the town I would keep running no matter what anyone said, and everyone had long since accepted the sight of me running along the streets in my shorts.

It didn't take much street running there to get to the country roads. A minute or two and I was alone. I never felt so "together" as when I was alone on the dirt road over what was known as the Three Humps — a stretch where no one lived or drove.

And I found I was never so lonely as when I ran on the streets of the city. I couldn't run away from the traffic, hostile taunts or from stares that hurt as much as the words. I couldn't escape these no matter how far or fast I ran in the city. I got defensive about it. Instead of running along looking calmly inside myself, as I'd always done before, I kept looking around to see that no one was about to run me down or put me down. The harder I looked for trouble, the more I found.

I finally let the real and imagined hostility bully me off the streets. It was a long time before I was sure enough of myself to realize it didn't matter what the hell anyone else thought when they saw me run.

It's human nature to fear what you don't know. And fear grows to suspicion, suspicion to hate. I was alone in the city — alone against masses of faceless people I didn't know. All I knew about them was that I didn't like them. I suspected the worst of them and tried to make them go away by pretending they weren't there.

I hid from people. I ran on the golf course before dawn or after sunset to keep from being seen. I walked to the track fully clothed and only stripped down to shorts when hidden by the deserted stadium. Running in the darkness or doing laps on the track wasn't much fun, but it was better than putting up with hostile crowds.

College running wasn't much better. This was the big-time. The school's team traveled around the country, racing against top competition, before big crowds. The coach's philosophy was, "Second place ain't worth a damn." His method of drawing the most from his runners was to match them against each other every day. It was an every-man-for-himself, survival-of-the-fittest situation.

I tried it for a year — looking at everyone else as a competitor, racing everyone all the time — but it was hopeless. I wasn't made to take running seriously or to fight for my running life every day.

The coach leaned back in his swivel chair, with his fingers laced behind his head. His prematurely gray hair might have given him a fatherly look. But the way that hair was cut — down to the scalp — and his beaked nose and piercing eyes blended in the unbending look of a Marine colonel.

I'd been in his office a hundred times before. I knew every picture and poster on the walls and could read the unanswered letters on the desk upside down. I usually liked being here. But this time I was anxious and stuttering.

I was telling the coach how I felt about running. As I poured out my story, he looked puzzled and skeptical. I told him everything. Why I thought I'd broken down. How I wanted to change my running. How I'd be giving up my scholarship if he'd let me change. I was talking down his values, but he heard me out.

"Well," he finally said, "it looks like you're determined to go ahead with this plan of yours. There's not much I can

144

do to stop you. It's an unusual request, you understand. I've had runners try to get out of work before, for all kinds of reasons. But it's always been because they were fed up with running. You seem eager to get on with it."

I nodded.

He leaned forward in his chair, put his arms on the desk and stared at me. "I guess you know that I can't give you any special favors. I'll let you train on your own if you want. But if you want to compete with the team, I want to see you in here every day to tell me what you're doing. I want you running every one of our time-trials. You'll go to meets *only* if you prove yourself there. If your performances drop, I'll have no choice but to leave you home."

I nodded again.

"Frankly," he said, "I don't give this plan of yours much hope. I've never seen a runner yet who succeeded on his own. Maybe you'll be different, but I doubt it."

I mumbled something.

"This may sound strange," Coach said, "but I think I know your trouble. You like to run too well. It doesn't bother you to lose because you like running so much. The reason you may never be a winner is that you don't mind losing. That attitude will keep you going for years and years, I'm sure. But it won't do you and us much good here and now."

Coach pushed back from his desk and stood up to see me out. He put his hand on my shoulder and said, "I think you're throwing away a great future in running. But apparently you're determined, so go ahead."

My running took the turn for the better that I knew it would. And the price of going my own way was about as

145

I'd expected: isolation, misunderstanding and some hostility.

Because I ran my way, I was different. The other runners on the team ran in a pack. I ran by myself. They ran by the coach's schedule. I ran on my own. They ran to the pace of the race. I ran what seemed like my best rate and more or less ignored the leaders.

They thought of themselves as normal, my teammates did. I was the odd one, so I was the subject of locker-room talk. I overheard my actions being explained a lot of ways: lazy, stand-offish, self-centered. I made no real attempt to explain myself since no one seemed too anxious to listen.

It's significant, perhaps, that all of those runners became ex-runners the day they left school. I might have gone the same way but for two coincidences: my small-town upbringing and road racing.

In the small town, there had been no coach telling me what to do. There had been no teammates to lean on for aid and comfort during training. I'd learned to run by myself — which may be an essential to survival in this sport. The responsibility for doing it ultimately is yours and yours alone. If you depend on others to carry you along, you'll usually end up being dropped.

I've never felt much of a need to hitch myself to other people when I run. Particularly to hyper-competitive, self-serious or faceless people. So it was a great relief to me when college ended. My obligation to coach and "team" were finished, and I was free to turn to an entirely different kind of running. Road running.

Its style wasn't anything like that of college track. That had been an extension of the city — an impersonal rat race. Running on the roads was more like living in a small town.

A slower, friendlier, more casual attitude prevailed. The people were closer to each other, I think, because there weren't so many of them and because competition had a different definition in long runs.

My good friend Bob Deines explained this atmosphere in *Distance Running News* after he set a 50-mile record.

"Long races seem to facilitate, more than the short ones, the definition of 'success' or 'winning' in personal terms. Although there was still some of the usual 'worship-the-winner' ritual after this 50-mile, it did not seem as dominant as in most shorter events. Here, in the really long runs, there is enough personal accomplishment in just finishing the race so that there is less of a need to look to the winner to identify with a sense of success.

"When each runner crosses the finish line, he knows that he has finished his own personal struggle, and he knows what he has done without anyone else telling him. The almighty stopwatch loses some of its power. Each individual can define his own success in his own terms."

But it was too good to last in this form. Other people — lots of others — learned the secret, and road running lost much of its old personality. In short, it grew up and left behind its child-like, play-like quality. Road running changed simply because it got crowded. And even good people in crowds become oppressive.

Five years earlier, almost to the day, I ran in California for the first time at almost this same spot. I was innocent yet, and I saw San Francisco's waterfront through innocent eyes. The Embarcadero didn't look the same now because I was no longer the same.

The city looked weary from trying to keep pace with the growth around it. So did the sport I was in. California

147

and running, two things I'd come here to combine, were showing the wear and tear of growing up too fast.

For most of its life, this race was called the Cross-City. It was a nice event that had attracted a few dozen hard-core distance runners since the time of the great earthquake. These runners didn't cause more than a brief ripple on the surface of city life.

Then the *Examiner*, a San Francisco newspaper, took over the race and changed its name to "Bay to Breakers." The paper gave the race publicity, and publicity drew crowds. This Sunday morning, the Examiner said on its front page, "2000 Entered in Bay-Breakers." The writer called it the biggest footrace in the history of mankind, but the size spoiled it for me.

Races offered two things — aloneness and togetherness — and this one had neither. "Aloneness" isn't the same thing as loneliness. Aloneness is getting close to yourself, getting acquainted with yourself by turning your eyes inward during an act you think is important. Races usually gave me that feeling.

"Togetherness" isn't melting into a mass of people. It is reaching out and touching other persons who have shared the same experiences, and racing experiences usually could be shared this way. But not here. There were so many people that the persons were lost and lonely in the crowd.

Because of its size, the race lost most of the features which usually justified this kind of effort-investment for me. A race had a clearly defined start and finish, with a clear stretch of road in between. The only obstacles were the ones I set up myself. At the end, there was a time and a place, a straightforward verdict.

This race had none of that. It wasn't a race at all, but a human wave rolling across San Francisco. I wasn't running.

148

I was being carried along, with no choice about whether to keep moving or not, to speed up or slow down. I was bobbing across the city, just one more head floating on the wave that covered four lanes of highway and spilled over to the sidewalks.

There was no feeling of uniqueness, and yet at the same time no feeling of community. I saw hundreds of faces, nearly all of them blank and without names to go with them. I stood shivering in my shorts as the ocean breeze sucked up my sweat and took the warmth with it. There were 2000 runners, and I couldn't find one I knew well enough to ask for a ride back to the start. The crowd dwindled, leaving me looking for friendly faces and seeing only the garbage that all of these people had left behind.

For a combination of reasons, only one being disgust with oversized fields, I quit going to races after that. Part of it was injuries. I was finally starting to see that racing too often was hurting me. Part of it was that I wasn't myself anymore. If anyone picked me out of the crowd, it wasn't me they were seeing — Joe Henderson, just another runner — but Joe Henderson, editor. I was a symbol, not a person. Before, after, even during races I was sometimes praised for my work, more often complained to about everything from typographical errors to mail service.

The negative things had something to do with my slipping away from the road racing scene—but not nearly so much as one big positive factor which I'd never experienced before. Group running. Not racing against other people, but running with them. Cooperating, not competing.

Never had there been anything like this, mainly because I could never find anyone in step with my way of running.

149

In high school, there had been no one else who ran at all. No one outside the school season or off the track, anyway — and most of my running was at other times and places. So I ran alone.

I was still alone in college — both because I was an "outsider" from the team and because I did most of my running long and on the roads. Not many Iowans in the early '60s had heard of Arthur Lydiard and what his New Zealanders were doing with "marathon training."

Then I came to California. People here had heard of Lydiard, and the better runners were training his way — 100 miles a week on the roads at 6-7 minute mile pace. I wouldn't or couldn't do that much or go as fast, so I was still alone.

This was okay most of the time. Running alone is the best way to see and think. But fatigue — the deep-down tiredness that comes of running more than an hour or two — deadens the senses and brings boredom. The longest runs are hard to do alone. Time drags.

I found myself skipping the long weekend run which is a traditional part of the Lydiard system and going to a race instead. I needed a human crutch to draw strength-building distance out of myself, and when I couldn't find it for training runs I was substituting strength-draining racing.

Just when I was getting run down from racing and a little bit fed up with what went with it, I fell in with The Group. It was spring, 1972, when we started meeting for long runs. The day of the run has changed since then, from Sunday to Saturday. The starting time and place are different. We don't run as far or as fast as we did at the start. I'm the only one left from the original group, and I was away from it for half a year. But The Group has gone on, as if it has a life of its own.

16. Talking

Leave it to a German to subject something as spontaneous as group running to sociological analysis and to apply rules to it. The method and the language Arnd Kruger uses to describe his group leave me cold. Yet his is the best description I've seen of why and how runners work together.

Kruger writes the obvious at the start: "The style of training that many runners now do may contribute to this tendency (to group running). The long, steady runs are especially suited to group effort. This kind of training is more pleasant psychically and runners cover more miles more comfortably than they do alone."

So we might call this Principle Number One: Runners group up for a practical, even selfish reason — to do more, more easily.

Principle Number Two is just as obvious: The group must have a set meeting place and time, on a regular day or days. That way, there's no need to do any "organizing" before each run.

Principle Three: The group is rather small, normally 5-7 members with similar abilities and ambitions. The membership is not so fixed as to keep new people from joining in.

Four: The group has an informal but generally agreed-upon leader who, in Kruger's words, "determines running direction and pace. This includes the procedure that when individuals run ahead and take the 'wrong' direction, they recognize the authority of the leader, to the extent that they turn back and follow him... In a group without such a leader, there is always the danger of overstressing. Best results come from cooperation in these runs rather than from competitive training."

The last paragraph pretty much covers the fifth principle, which is that these are training runs to be carried out at paces and distances well within the "comfort" range. They are not races.

Principle Number Six is more of a test: Does the group stay together and keep talking all the way? If it does, it is working well.

If this is John, it must be three o'clock Friday afternoon. Several Johns run with The Group, but John Ladniak is the only one who calls. And he calls every Friday at three.

"Are you going to be there tomorrow morning?" he asks.

"Plan to," I say.

He knows the answer as well as I know the question. We're almost always there, and a call for confirmation isn't necessary. John and I have run together on Saturday mornings, same time and place, since 1974. I suspect he calls for the same reason I like to get his calls. They bring Friday afternoon quitting time that much closer.

John is an exception to two of Arnd Kruger's "rules of group running." He's the only one in our group who checks to see if there's to be a run. The others accept it on faith and tradition that we'll meet in the Foothill College parking lot, rain or shine, cold or hot, spring or fall, at eight o'clock. At least one other person will always be there.

152

Also, with John as with me, the Saturday group run is an end in itself — not a step to better racing as it is with most of the others. John averages about one race a year and doesn't even take that one very seriously.

"After 15 years of competitive tennis," he says, "I'm ready for something more relaxed. This run is the highlight of my week. It gets out all the crap that has built up in me all week. This is all I need from my running. I don't have to bother with all the hassle of racing."

Nonetheless, it is racing which inspires former joggers and ex-middle distance jocks to go longer. The lure of the marathon first brings almost all of them to The Group and keeps them coming back. They wouldn't come out without it.

As a race, the marathon is vastly overrated. Running 26 miles 385 yards is of no more intrinsic value than going 15 1/2 or 9 1/3. But what is important about the marathon is that it's a goal which changes people's life-styles. And other long runs don't have the power to do that. So if the marathon is the only carrot which will get them to do the hour a day needed to keep them whole, I won't hesitate to dangle it in front of anyone.

Every Sunday at the Fun-Runs our company sponsors, I have the same conversation. An older, slightly overweight man or a knob-kneed teenager, says, "I'm kind of thinking I'd like to run that marathon coming up in a couple of months."

I say, "Good. How much running are you doing?"

"Not enough, probably. Maybe three or four miles a day."

I know that means two or three miles on the running days, and at least a couple of days a week with nothing at all. I say, "If you want to be sure of getting through the marathon rather comfortably, you really should be doing twice that much, or a little more. Seven to 10 miles a day on the average, including one run a week of about twice that far. That long run is very important."

The runner winces at these distances.

"Don't worry," I tell him. "This isn't as bad as it sounds. For one thing, you don't have to worry about speed. Just cover the distances however you can."

"I can make the daily ones," he says, "but it's the long one that scares me. God, I've never been over seven miles."

Here comes the pitch: "It helps if you run with a group. It takes your mind off the distance. As a matter of fact, we have a group which meets here every Saturday. We go 12-15 miles, nice and easy. Why don't you join us some week?"

In a way, I'm conning this runner. "Nice and easy" is a relative term which may apply to veterans of The Group but seldom to newcomers without a long-distance background. For the novice, the Saturday run can be frightening and discouraging. There's no break-in period. It's 12-15 miles the first day. Cold turkey.

Still, it's better now than it once was. For a time in 1975, The Group showed some of the growing pains that had been bothering me about distance *racing*. "Growing," "long" and "racing" are the key words here, in fact.

The Group had gone along for years with an average of five people. Not always the same five, but with about five each week. Then, suddenly, there were 15 or 20. The Group had lost its closeness.

Some more ambitious people came than had been there before. I have nothing against the ambitious runners themselves. But they put a severe strain on The Group by

154

pushing both the distance and pace to new and higher levels. Instead of 12-15 miles, we started going 15-20. Instead of a gentle 8-8 1/2 minutes a mile, we started at eight, dropped to 7 1/2 after a few miles, then to seven and faster yet at the end. That's what happened with the people in front, anyway. Others of us couldn't keep up.

The disintegration of The Group started on two winter Saturdays, and was almost complete by the fall. So it wasn't a sudden collapse which anyone could see coming and protect against. Rather, it was a slow, crumbling erosion that kind of sneaked up on us.

I was responsible for the first of the bad days. It was a frosty morning around Christmas. The mountain rim to the west of Foothill had a light blanket of snow — something which only comes once or twice a winter here.

In half-jest, I asked, "Anyone want to go to Skyline?" That's a 2000-foot vertical climb in nine miles. And the leg-pounding run back down is almost as bad as the climb.

There was an answering chorus of yeahs, sures, okays and hey-greats. All mountains have a fatal lure built into them.

My stubby legs are built for hill-climbing. "You're the only person I know," someone in The Group said, "who runs the same pace uphill and down. If we threw you off of one of the cliffs on the way to Skyline, you'd probably fall at eight minutes per mile."

I didn't seem to be going very fast. Just ambling along, talking with John, the non-racer who is also a hill-climbing fanatic. Then on a sweeping bend, we looked back and down, and saw individual runners — many of them now walking — stretched out for half a mile.

I didn't know most of them, because this was a heavy growth period for The Group and at least a half-dozen of

155

the runners were new this week. Only one or two of them ever came back after this beginning.

A little later that winter, a well-meaning man who was far too advanced for our people led The Group on its worst run ever.

He called me on Friday, asking, "Will your group be running tomorrow?"

"Sure," I said. "We always run. But I can't be there."

"Oh. Well, I had in mind showing these people something different. Something special. Do you think they'd be interested?"

"Go ahead and ask," I said. "I'm just one of The Group and can't speak for everyone."

I started hearing horror stories the next afternoon and would keep hearing them for months to come.

"We started," someone said, "by going straight up this MF-ing mountain for four or five miles. And this guy who got us there was carrying his camera. Every half-mile or so, he'd sprint up ahead, and stop and take our picture because his girl friend was with us.

"We figured, God, if this girl's here, it can't get much worse. But come to find out later that she was doing 70 or 80 miles a week and was in as good shape as he was."

The run climbed to Skyline Drive then went along the ridge — on trails. (Someone told me, "We kept going through private property with signs which said, 'Trespassers will be shot on sight.' ") Then they plunged quickly back down into the valley.

The people who came back the next week were still psyched-out, angry and sore. One of the regulars didn't make it back that week, or for a long time to come.

156

Hollis Logue III writes outrageous satire for Runner's World, much of which never gets published because the conservative editor thinks it is too wild. But Hollis keeps writing it down and sending it in — his record is three articles in one day, mailed in the same envelope — because he could no more stop that than stop talking. He's a prodigious talker whose verbal stories are, if anything, more outrageous than his written ones.

Hollis goes way back with The Group. He started running when we were still at Stanford, and there aren't many of us left from the small band. He liked to talk during those early runs about the marathons he would race. He did enter and finish one in good time for a start. But I suspect Hollis came on Saturday mornings more for the chance to try out his stories on a captive and receptive audience.

He was with The Group that Saturday when the stranger led them off into the mountains. Hollis called that afternoon to tell me with his usual adornments what a nightmare the run had been. He mentioned in passing that the run had given him a pain in the knee. That pain grew so severe that it cost Hollis four months of running and hundreds of dollars in podiatrist bills.

He called often during that time, trying to find a sympathetic ear. His withdrawal symptoms, laments over lost running, fears that he would never run again were pretty routine—except that he said in every call, "You know the one thing I miss the most is not the racing, not even the getting out and clearing my head every day. It's the Saturday runs. I took them for granted when I had them, but now..."

"What has happened?" Hollis Logue III asked when he came back to The Group the following fall. "The run seems

157

so much faster and more serious than it used to. I feel like I don't belong. Is it just me and the fact that I'm not in the shape I was before, or have things really changed?"

The Group probably never was as good as Hollis had imagined in his time away. His return may have been a little disappointing, like making a nostalgic visit to one's hometown and having the reality of it stamp out a dream. But The Group had changed — so slowly and subtly that I couldn't see it happening from week to week, yet so dramatically to Hollis, whose views were separated by many months.

We were climbing a long, bald hill above Stanford University. The path could be seen for a mile ahead. Hollis and I had been alone at the back for a long time.

I pointed up the hill and said, "Look at that. That answers your question about what has happened to us."

Off in the distance, silhouetted by the morning sun, were lone runners, one every hundred yards.

"It isn't our group any more," I said. "It isn't even a group at all, but 15 individuals running a race against each other."

Hollis nodded seriously. "Let's see what we can do to bring The Group back together. I don't want to lose it again."

The Group needed a leader to bring it back together. I don't fancy myself to be one, never wanted to be one. But in the early days I had inherited the job. The honor had nothing to do with comparative ability or with what anyone else imagined I knew about running. I'd lived and run in these hills for years and knew the way through them, that was all. The others let me lead so they wouldn't get lost.

But I've always been the slowest trainer in town. The new people in The Group liked to go a lot faster. They grew impatient with my gentle amble and sped away from it as soon as they learned the new territory.

Since The Group had never had the strong, acknowledged leader which Arnd Kruger says is essential, we were like lambs following the fastest runner of the week — who was going too fast and too far for almost everyone else.

I would like to say I exercised wise leadership and brought the wandering flock back together. But it isn't so. We did regroup, but I had little to do with it — with a couple of minor and subtle exceptions. Mostly, we came together again because Hollis Logue and I weren't the only ones who thought that running with each other was more fun than racing alone.

Not that there's anything wrong with either being alone or racing. But this isn't the time or place for thinking or testing. The Group's run gives a rare chance to talk, and when that goes The Group is gone.

We all seemed to sense this and made the necessary adjustments without being conscious that we were making them. The Group straightened itself out on its own, as if it had a mind apart from those of the individuals who were it.

First, and probably most important, the fastest of the competitors who had been setting The Group's pace and style for several months grew bored with the plodding and carefree spirit which still, somehow was dominant. They drifted away.

Next — and this is where I had a subtle influence — the distance came down a little. At 15-20 miles in 2-2 1/2 hours, it had been too long and tiring for most of us. Ideally, it should be about twice the daily average. Much longer than that and it would take all week to recover. The Group's runners rarely average more than 5-7 miles a day, so I guided us on courses of 12-15 miles.

The people who wanted more began coming a half-hour earlier and taking a "pick-up lap" of 3-5 miles before joining the main body of The Group at eight o'clock. Or they added on a few miles at the end.

At the same time, we started attracting people who wanted to do less. A woman named Barbara said, "There are lots of us who would love to come along with you on Saturdays. But there's no way we can go as far as you do. We'd like to work up to it eventually, but now we can only do about half as much."

The "Break-in Group" now turns back at halfway.

The regular Group itself has split two or three ways — but it's a healthy kind of split, not the destructive one which had happened before.

The comfortable group size is about five. When it gets bigger than that, it sub-divides automatically. It isn't planned that way. No one is assigned permanently to one sub-group or another. Yet, as we go along, clusters of slower and faster and sometimes in-between runners develop. Everyone goes to the one which best matches his or her pace and personality.

Years ago, I was foolish for a while and almost drove myself out of running. But looking back on it now, I don't regret the time lost to injury because it taught me things I wouldn't have known otherwise. It forced me to look closely at myself and what I was doing wrong — at what was really healthy and important in running.

I appreciate running so much more now after almost losing it. And the same is true of The Group. It's better and stronger now that it has weathered a crisis. The traditions of the Saturday run have survived and grown.

The meeting place and time — always the same.

The courses — one of four standard routes which every regular knows by a simple code word: "Dog," "Park," "Hill," "Stanford."

The split — the automatic sub-dividing into smaller, closer groups.

The talk — stiff, ritualistic banter at first, then as the body warms up and begins to flow so does the conversation.

The breakfast — a tradition borrowed from the Southern California "Breakfast Club." The runners there go all-out, with one runner treating all the others at his home or a restaurant. We settle for buying our own Egg McMuffin and orange juice at McDonald's. It's the people, not the place, which make Saturday mornings special.

17. Testing

To race — to compete with other runners or just with the clock and the distance — is to beat yourself up both physically and psychologically.

Racing hurts. There is fear for hours to days before, sometimes intense pain during and hangover fatigue after every race which goes to the limit. And it can't be called a good race unless it pushes limits.

The fear, pain and fatigue pass rather quickly. So does the glow of having passed the test. Unfortunately, the mental and physical injuries which are always a risk in racing don't go away as quickly. So the legacy of racing is often chronic pain and disappointment.

This gamble is more easily lost than won. Yet after losses which include one foot operation and more than a dozen other periods of being a near-invalid because of racing, I'm still a gambler. And I tell other runners to gamble... at least once... if only to help them appreciate how nice the other runs feel.

I fully realize by saying this that I'm contradicting much of the advice that this book is built around. For instance, racing contributes little or nothing to physical fitness — and more often works against it. It exaggerates deadline-chasing, hyper-competitive, "Type-A" tendencies. The pace is too hard to be meditative, creative or addictive. Yet I see values in running to the limits — so long as the amount and type of races are carefully controlled.

The values:

1. It satisfies a risk-taking urge that most of us have but can seldom express in not-too-threatening ways.

2. It unleashes the competitor inside us who gets frustrated if he can't exercise occasionally, but who will devour us if allowed to roam too freely.

3. It helps hook people on running who otherwise would have trouble getting through the habit-forming period. It may not contribute directly to addiction, but it is a goal which excites runners enough to train in addictive doses.

4. It is good for the ego, giving insecure runners something they can take pride in and teaching overconfident ones some humility.

5. It completes the running picture. The three parts are "solo" runs (where the most important thing going on is thinking), "social" runs (talking) and "speed" runs (testing).

However, these should not be thought of as three equal parts — each taking up 33 1/3 percent of a runner's time. The priorities, for a number of reasons outlined earlier in the book, are (1) solo, (2) social and (3) speed. I recommend a ratio of five solo miles to one social; at least 20 of those two for each mile of racing. Among other things, this 20:1 ratio insures complete recovery between races.

The results — times and finishing places — from races have a certain temporary value. I wouldn't be honest if I didn't say I'm proud of them for a few days after successfully beating myself up in a race. But as time passes, I'm prouder that I was able to stand the beating and come back to run again.

My first coach, Dean Roe, didn't know much about training methods. In 1958, he probably hadn't heard yet about intervals and fartlek. But he knew about adolescent psychology.

Coach Roe's method was simple: race every day. He lined up all the 100-yard dashmen every afternoon for a 100-yard dash down the middle of the football field. The quarter-milers sprinted two laps around the field, which passed as the school's track. The half-milers raced five halves a week.

I was a half-miler, and I probably raced that distance 50 times my freshman year. It wasn't the wisest way to train, but it did wonders for a shaky young ego.

Like most 14-year-olds, I needed confidence more than conditioning. I was rather fit because... well, fitness comes with being 14. You can do all sorts of foolish things at that age and have the resiliency to bounce back. But I stood on what marathoner-writer Kenny Moore once called "the uncertain sands of adolescent society." Moore wrote, "Perhaps the clear delineation of excellence found in running provides a solidarity that balances the uncertain sands."

Success is where you find it. I found mine on a 220-yard chalk line around a small-town football field. Here, I could measure myself against other runners and against my own times, and here I saw I was measuring up rather well. But I needed regular reassurance that this was so. At 14, my confidence had a lifespan of about one day, and Dean Roe knew just how to renew it.

A lot of years and a lot of races have passed since then. I have changed, and so has my running. Both have matured, I hope. I don't have to chase after people and times any more to keep myself going. I can enjoy a wandering running, unranked and unmeasured.

I don't race as often as I used to, both out of choice and necessity. The years and tens of thousands of miles have left me too brittle for that. My infrequent racing isn't as serious or as fast as it once was, but it's just as vital.

Running as I do, apparently going in endless circles from nowhere to nowhere, races are important benchmarks. Now, they don't so much show progress or slippage as they tell who I am.

Without a race every so often, I lose the sense of awe at what I can do when I press myself, and at the same time I lose my humility. I forget that racing can make the impossible possible and the possible impossible. Only here can I end up running faster than I ever thought I could or unable to cover a distance I've gone a thousand times before.

Every race is a question, and I never know until the last yards what the answer will be. That's the lure of racing.

To race is to take chances. It's a chance to win something that seems important or to do something that barely seems possible — and at least an equal chance of hurting yourself or making an ass of yourself in public. We race *because* of this gamble, not in spite of it.

Races, like all risk-taking exercises, are emotional and defy logical explanation. I've written sane, rational advice about racing but don't practice much of it. It all was written from a safe distance away. When I'm racing, I'm as irrational as the next person, because racing itself is irrational.

Racing turns people who are normally afraid of their own reflections into athletes who run until they can't stand up. It turns meek, bookish types into hot-eyed competitors who will run up their friends' backs to gain places. Racing drives them farther and faster than they ever could go without being turned on emotionally.

An interviewer said to Frank Shorter, the 1972 Olympic marathon champion, "Most people can't even run one five-minute mile, and you're able to string 26 of them together. Does that ever boggle your mind?"

Shorter answered, "Yeah, I can't just sit here and decide that I'm going to put on my shoes and go out to run even 15 miles at a five-minute pace. You just have to be in the race situation. Getting pulled along is the big thing."

The race situation sometimes exposes hidden potential. But it also bares one's weaknesses for everyone to see. Racing brings out the best and worst in people.

If you rank competitors on a scale of one to 10 according to their killer instincts, I'm about a two. I'm not guessing at this. I have the word of sports psychologist Dr. Bruce Ogilvie. He tested me several years ago and concluded that I'm better suited for bird-watching than for competitive athletics.

When I race, I run for time and not position. But to get the fastest possible time, I need other people around. I need them to push and pull me along — but only from a distance. When they get too close, they upset my concentration and rhythm. Then I get irritated with them for not playing by my rules.

My rules are that no one sets out to stab anyone else in the back. No one is in the race to beat anyone else, but only to get the best from himself or herself. This way, everyone can be a winner.

166

Tactics have no place in my rules, because tactics have little to do with running at one's best. They're only involved with running better than the next person — not so much outrunning him as outsmarting him. This makes racing a symbolic little chess match at best and a street fight at worst.

I don't know their names, so I call them Splat and Sprint for the way they run. I've never seen Splat before. But from the start of this race, I hear him. I go fast up the first hill and am alone for a hundred yards or so. But I hear his feet slapping against the pavement: "Schplatt! Schplatt! Schplatt!"

Splat comes alongside, so close he bumps my elbow, and stays there. His tactic is to run stride for stride with me no matter what... which is distracting since he is 6'2" and I'm 5'6" and our strides don't match.

Sprint and I have raced before. Last time, he hung in my shadow for .99 of a mile then squirted past at the end as if beating me was a big deal. His eyes are on my back now. I can feel them.

I try to separate myself from these two as we go downhill. I move away. Then at the bottom, a sudden cramping pain grabs my calf muscle.

A rational man would think, "Something's wrong, and it can only get worse if I keep going. I'll stop now."

My thought is, "Gotta keep going. Gotta keep this lead. Can't let these guys catch me now. Maybe if I ignore this pain, it'll go away."

I limp up the next hill and then down, holding pace but looking more and more like a cheating race walker as I fall back on my heels to ease the pain.

167

I look around. Racers aren't supposed to do that, but I'm scared. Splat has fallen back. But Sprint is glaring at me. My worried look turns on his kick.

I make a token spurt and hold him off by a step. The timer yells out some numbers. I don't hear and don't care. I can't put full weight on the right leg, but it doesn't matter. I'll worry about that tomorrow. I've won. I've broken all my rules and feel good about it. Damn good.

This is the value of racing: a chance to take chances, to do crazy, impulsive things. The body may not be made to take the strain of racing. But the need to take risks is bred into us. In a world with most of the risks programmed out, we have to make up ways to take chances. Mine are in races.

My everyday running is safe and conservative. I never take chances there. I rarely hurt. I feel good about it but in a different way than I feel about races. I feel a mild glow after my morning runs. Races, however, are a total physical-emotional jolt that only comes with throwing myself into a great unknown. I don't need this as often as before, but I still need it.

18. Training

If ever there was a candidate for "least likely to succeed," I would have been it. When I started running as a freshman in high school, there was no sign that I had any business in the sport or would stay in it for long.

My high school was small. We had no track, unless we stretched a point and called the 220-yard chalk line around the football field a "track." We did have a track team but in name only. The coach coached everything. Football, boys' and girls' basketball, track. He was tiring by spring and was ready to coast instead of coach.

He felt this way about track: "If you want to run, fine. I'll come out with my stopwatch and time you. But if you don't want to run, that's fine, too. I can stay inside and drink coffee and grade papers. If you want to go to meets, I'll be glad to take care of the paperwork for you and to see that you get there and back. But if you don't want to go, I won't force you. I won't mind having my nights and weekends free."

Occasionally, the school would win a place in one of the natural-ability events. But never in anything that took training. For the few runners with any interest in preparing for races, the coach's method was quite basic. Run several time-trials a week. If you were a quarter-miler, you'd dash off a quarter. If you were a miler, you'd go a mile. Nothing more, nothing less. No warmup. No repeats. No warmdown.

169

I ran my first race on no training. And I'd dropped out of it after one lap of a mile. I decided then I'd rather be a half-miler. I started the coach's time-trials. Always half-miles.

I got to like running and wanted to do more of it. So I added several easy miles on the roads, some before and some after the daily trial, some more on weekends. By the end of the next season, I was in the state meet in the two-mile relay. The next year, I did more miles and fewer trials and placed in the state in the mile.

As a junior and senior, I went to a new school in a new town, eight miles from home. I usually ran home from school because I could beat the bus that way. That distance plus a few races gave me six state championships in cross-country and track.

I'm not straining to pat myself on the back. None of that is intended or deserved. Remember, this was among the small-class schools in a rather backward track state, and it was almost 15 years ago. The times I ran then wouldn't win most dual meets now.

But the point I'm making is that I instinctively hit upon a simple and enjoyable way of running which at the same time took me about as far as I could go on my limited talent. Most importantly, I was anxious to keep running, not looking for a stopping place as so many high school graduates are.

So I went away to college. I signed on with a coach who knew just about everything about training methods. He gave me workouts so complicated that I couldn't figure out where I'd been and where they were leading me. No more easy miles on the roads combined with a few races and trials. That was too primitive. It may have worked in high school, but it wasn't good enough for the big-time.

Maybe not. But I didn't belong in the big-time, either, and I needed something more "primitive." In the first year of college, my mile time went from 4:22 to 4:50, my three-mile from about 15 minutes to more than 16.

Earlier, I'd stumbled onto the right combination of endurance and speed — a torrent of distance and a dribble of fast stuff. I didn't know what the combination was, so I stumbled in and out of it a half-dozen more times until I finally broke the code a couple of years ago.

I relaxed after the first year of college racing — dropping pretenses of becoming an Olympic champion and settling again on lots of miles and a few races. My times went back down, to faster than they'd ever been.

I got ambitious again, sped more and got hurt.

I relaxed, turned to a kind of running that came to be known as LSD (long slow distance) and was able to go long and fast again in my rare distance races.

I raced more often. Performance leveled off and then slowed. I was tired most of the time. And sore. I ignored the tiredness and soreness, and it developed into illness and injury. I couldn't race any more. And then I couldn't run any more.

I was in the sorriest mental-physical shape in my life. Only then, out of desperation, did I figure out the formula I'd been on during every successful, healthy, happy running period since the start—and off of during the down times.

It's as simple as this.

Goal: Keep moving.

Means: 1. Keep healthy; 2. Keep fresh; 3. Keep loose; 4. Keep hungry.

Recipe: At least 10 parts of easy running to one part hard.

The only valid test of a running method is, "Can I keep running with it?" If not, no coach, no German physiologist can make it work. Throw away the schedule if it won't pass your road test.

The way to keep going is to eliminate the negatives. If you want to run tomorrow morning and the next day and as many days into the future as you can imagine, and if you are able to do it, you've already won.

Stay healthy. Any method of running which hurts can't be helping much. What have you gained if you run 150 miles this week and are too sore to run at all for the next month?

Stay fresh. Chronic fatigue leads to injuries and, worse, the feeling that you can't face the next morning. What have you gained if you run five-minute miles today but can't run 10-minute pace for the next week?

Stay loose. Run your running, don't let it run you. A schedule is a guide, not a holy order chiseled in stone. Slavery to a pre-set routine causes you to run too much when you don't feel like it and not enough when you feel ready for more. Trust your feelings.

Stay hungry. Hungry in the psychological sense, meaning that something is always left unexplored. Keep an appetite for tomorrow. Don't stuff yourself so much on running that it makes you sick.

The key to all of this — avoiding injuries and nagging fatigue, inflexibility and disinterest — may be the ratio of easy to hard runs, slow to fast ones.

I had no idea what it might be until two wiser men tipped me off. Independently, Arthur Lydiard and Ernst van

Aaken came to much the same formula. They discovered it years before I realized what they meant.

Lydiard, in New Zealand, said that endurance miles should outnumber speed miles 10-1. Van Aaken, a German medical doctor and coach, was even more conservative. His ratio was 20:1 or more.

I'd listed every race and every run in a loose-leaf diary-type binder. Since 1966, all of my running had been one extreme or the other—easy or all-out. So my own running-racing balance was easy to figure out. Two patterns jumped out of the mass of statistics.

1. I raced best when I raced 5 percent of my miles (20:1 ratio).

2. I raced worst, was tired, sick and hurt most often when I raced 10 percent or more of the total.

There may have been a point down around two percent or less where I lost sharpness from not racing enough. I couldn't tell. I'd never been down that low. My problem has always been in the other direction. It was a problem of recovery. I seem to need 10-20 recovery miles for every all-out one.

Think of it as money in the bank. Gentle endurance running adds to the account, and hard speed work drains it. Anyone who has balanced a checkbook knows that money flows out a lot faster than it comes in. The same is true in running. Endurance builds slowly. Speed takes away quickly. So the trick is to keep a large reserve account built up—to have enough endurance on hand to meet emergencies and then to make up all deficits before withdrawing again.

This is the reason for running no more than one fast mile in every 10. It takes the easy 10 to replace what was lost in the one.

How fast is "easy"? I can't say. It's something you have to feel. It's set by an internal clock which is quite delicate.

Yoga uses the concept of "playing the edges." Stretch slowly to the border between comfort and discomfort, then hold that position. You can't improve flexibility without maximum stretch. But improvement stops and strain begins if you push on into pain.

This happens with running too. You run along the edge between comfort and discomfort. Run at a pace which feels right. Stretch but don't strain. Trust your instincts to tell you what's right.

How far to go? Trust your feelings there, too, but with one qualification. This has to do with racing distances. Run enough to handle the longest one. How much is "enough"? The minimum is one-third of the racing distance (or time, if you keep records as I do, by time instead of distance) per day. Not necessarily every day, but at least averaging that one-third.

For instance, I typically average a little less than an hour a day. That puts my upper limit at about two hours. I should be able then to handle any race through 20 miles, but my marathon — which takes me all of three hours— might fall apart at 22-23 miles.

This upper limit of distance is called the "collapse point." Beyond it lies pain and disappointment. I know. I've been there many times. Since I don't care to go again, I now make sure I have enough distance background for any race I run.

The best way to prepare for racing is to race. Racing calls out hidden abilities you can't get out of yourself any other way. You can't duplicate in normal speedwork the effort of racing because the excitement and shot of adrenaline aren't there. People like me who dread and despise interval work, time-trials, that kind of thing and will have nothing to do with them, still look ahead eagerly to races.

I get so worked up about them, in fact, that I'm tempted to run too many — to race the next time before I'm completely over the last one. This isn't much of a problem for a miler, who recovers quickly and needs to race one, two or even three times a week at peak season. But it's an increasing threat to a long distance man like me who has the chance to race twice a weekend but shouldn't do it more than once or twice a month.

As recently as a few years ago, I wasn't satisfied to do a few races well. I had to try them all. On consecutive weekends, I raced a marathon, 20 miles and 30 kilometers. I hurt my foot badly enough in the marathon to pull out after 15 miles. It still hurt the next week, but I raced anyway. It hurt worse the Sunday after that, but I ran again. It was the better part of two years before I raced normally again.

Since then, I've found and used my recovery-rebuilding timetable. I've learned that 10 easy miles after every hard one is a bare minimum. I'm hung-over from the race for at least that long. So I multiply the race distance or time by 10 and refuse to let myself go hard again until that quota is reached.

Racing 10 percent of the time is enough for me, and I suspect for anyone. And good racing, like all good running, is knowing how to hug the border between enough and too much. "Enough" keeps you going. "Too much" breaks you down.

19. Reflecting

John Steinbeck wrote in his book *Sweet Thursday*, "Looking back, you can usually find the moment of the birth of a new era, whereas when it happened it was one day hooked onto the tail of another."

Looking back, I can see many such days — days that look from this angle to spell dramatic changes. But when they were happening, they were just days more or less like the others around them.

I look back on three of those days in 1966. I see them now as significant anniversaries. But they weren't planned that way and didn't seem memorable at the time.

I (1) began writing for pay, (2) subscribed to a new running magazine, and (3) slowed down and lengthened my runs.

I took a job with a newspaper sports department because I couldn't find work in teaching. I signed up for *Distance Running News*, Bob Anderson's new publication, because I read everything available on running — and that wasn't much in 1966. I wanted to keep racing fast miles for several more years, but my increasingly fragile legs begged for a change. The choice had swung from fast or slow to slow or nothing.

The newspaper was dreary work. I wrote the fillers read only by the people who made the news. But I wrote them 20-30 times every night, which forced writing experience on me.

Track & Field News, my next stop, funneled the writing down from all sports to one. I stayed there three years, learning to write stories longer than a paragraph.

Meanwhile, Bob Anderson's magazine was growing. He changed the name to *Runner's World* and needed an editor, as he could no longer explore that whole world by himself. Bob wanted someone with experience in running and writing about it, willing to start at $75 a week. He didn't have a line of applicants at his door.

I took the job, since it was a chance to say things about running which other magazines weren't printing. Some of these were so obvious no one bothered to say them, some so far out that no one dared.

None of these things sound unusual now to runners trained on 1970s thinking. But to runners of five and 10 years ago, trained by high school and college teams and fed a diet of daily newspapers' worship-the-winner pap, the RW message was slightly revolutionary.

Not everyone can go fast, it said, but anyone can go long.

You can be as much a winner as anyone in a race, just by being there. Don't watch. Do!

If you don't care to race, that's okay, too. The mental and physical rewards of gentle, everyday running are as great as anything found at the finish line.

I started thinking this way only after my running slowed and lengthened in 1966. The change opened my eyes to the possibilities beyond fitness and beyond competition. It showed me a third level, above the other two, where running is fun — where running today and feeling good about it now is all I want and need.

The seeds that grew into this new view of running and into today's *Runner's World* were planted then — not only

177

in Des Moines, Iowa, and Manhattan, Kansas, but independently in scattered other places.

The seeds have blown across the land and sprouted more runners than I would have thought was possible in 1966. But mixed in with the healthy growth is some bad seed which can bring trouble if we don't weed it out early.

As a runner who pre-dates the "revolution," I'm happy with almost everything that has happened in the sport in the last 10 years. But I must say that a few trends disturb and even disgust me. I would like to help kill them before they grow out of control.

My old-fashionedness is showing, I know. And I know I shouldn't let these things bother me too much because they don't have to change my own running. But some of the directions running seems to be taking do bother me because I care about the sport and the people in it. I know what it can give, and in a way I feel responsible for pointing out the wrongs and playing up the rights which I see. One recent week's mail carried a lot of the wrongs.

It had to come to this I suppose. Officials announced an invitational Olympic Trial Marathon, with many of the men getting full expense money to race in Eugene. They'd earned the right to run there by going 2:20 or faster. Others under 2:23 could run if they found their own way to Oregon.

Long distance running finally had its semi-professional elite. We started in that direction in 1969 when the Boston Marathon set its first qualifying standard – the first such standard in U.S. road racing, which until then had been completely open.

The National AAU Marathon in Eugene in 1971 had a three-hour standard. It was the first entry limit on a national race. In 1972, the Olympic Trials barred anyone over 2:30. Never before had a Trials been anything but open.

In 1973, '74 and '75, U.S. invitational races began competing for top talent, and paying to get it. This hadn't been done in any big way before.

It surprised me in 1974 that there weren't more complaints — or at least expressions of dismay — when the *Los Angeles Times* put together a marathon with a $100 entry fee. The money was said to go to "charity," and there's no reason to think it didn't.

The slower runners, as usual, paid up. Some 50-60 of them plunked down $100 for the privilege of running on hot, smoggy streets for three or four hours.

Meanwhile, the top runners had their flights, motels and meals paid for. And rumors sneaked around that the leading men had been offered an extra $1000, $2000, $3000 — depending on the man and who was telling the story.

An official assured me the expense money didn't come from the charity pot. But that wasn't my main concern. My concern was with the precedent of charging one group of runners an exorbitant fee while giving another group a lavish bonus. This wasn't the simple, cheap sport I'd come to know.

All of this was leading to the 1976 Trials, where only 2:23 men would run and all would be subsidized. Where it will lead by 1980 and 1984, I don't want to guess.

A perverse side of human nature likes to watch suffering from a close but safe distance. The Romans entertained their crowds by putting gladiators and lions and Christians together in arenas. We do it with football players and race car drivers.

179

For pure, self-inflicted suffering, though, few events could rival the marathon-dance-type spectacles of the 1920s and 1930s. Back then, a huckster named C. C. Pyle organized runs for money across the United States, promising the finishers fame and fortune. A platoon of runners did the necessary suffering, but the promised dollars weren't waiting for them at the end. This is still one of the sorriest chapters in the history of the sport.

I like to think runners now are too intelligent to let themselves be used this way. But are they? This week, Dee Collins announced a 1970s version of the Bunion Derbies. Collins called this the Great American Marathon. It was to be run from Constitution Hall in Philadelphia to the Alamo in San Antonio, 1800 miles away. The contestants would go 30 miles a day for more than two months in the heat of summer.

Only women could compete. But promoters thought they'd get so many of them that state preliminaries would be needed to whittle down the field. The winner, you see, stood to make $50,000. Second-place money was $25,000, third $10,000, etc. It was enough to make some women think of renouncing their amateur status, and for some men to contemplate sex-change surgery...

Until they remembered how hard it is to run a single marathon in mid-summer in the humid East, Midwest and South. And they realized they'd be racing more than a marathon day after day, with no time to rest, recover and rebuild, for most of the summer.

It would be gruesome, and the media would eat it up. Lots of people love freak shows, and lots of people will make freaks of themselves for that kind of money.

As a sport grows, people who want attention have to do weirder and weirder things to get it. A marathon used to be enough. But now more than 5000 Americans run marathons each year. Runners don't usually run to be part of a crowd, so they try to break away from it — to do something unique.

A few do it by going faster and faster. But there aren't many Frank Shorters, and ability assigns most of us to a place in the faceless crowd. So some of us go longer and longer—50 kilometers, 24 hours, across the state, across the continent. But we're limited here by time and training. Not many of us can take off two or three months to cross the U.S., as Bruce Tulloh and others have done. And Ted Corbitt is a rare man who can stand the stress of 300-mile weeks or would try.

Others, who have neither the talent to run fast nor the time to run long, use their imaginations. The week's mail carried a disturbing story about an older marathoner who finished in 2:33. Trouble was, no one remembered seeing him at the start. None of the runners just before or after him ever saw him during the race. He wasn't checked through any of the five-mile points. He finished looking as if he'd just gone a couple of miles — which may be close to the truth.

Unfortunately, this wasn't the first time a distance runner let ambition and imagination run wild. A woman had us believing for a couple of years that she'd set a half-dozen world records in time-trials. She'd won a college scholarship with marks that she'd made only in her head.

If these and other cases like them were harmless pranks, done in fun, we could laugh them off. But these runners are dead serious. They want so much for their phony results to be real that they start believing them themselves. This reflects a dissatisfaction with who they are and what they can do.

A little dissatisfaction is a good thing. Wanting to change what we are is the essential motivation which turns us into different and better people. This is the kind of thinking which turns six-minute freshman milers into 4:30 runners as seniors. It makes 150-pound distance runners from former 200-pound non-athletes.

A deeper kind of dissatisfaction, though, eats away at the fabric of the sport and the spirit of its people. It's a gnawing need to grab for something which will always be out of reach. The people who cheat to get what they need end up cheating themselves out of the things which running can offer everyone at minimal cost.

Running is best at its simplest. To expand it too much, to control it too tightly, to complicate and make it too mechanical or scientific is to mock and pervert the basic, natural, freeing act of moving on foot.

The week's mail told of two perversions... well, let me call them unnecessary complications in deference to the well-meaning men behind them.

The first came from a man on the West Coast who breaks up the "monotony" of a run by taking along a jump-rope and skipping through his miles. He recently ran half the length of his state this way as a publicity stunt. He sent us an article urging other runners to jump rope to liven the dull routine.

I rejected the article, telling him, "To publish it would give the impression that something is wrong with running itself and that it needs an additive to be whole. I guess you could call me a purist. But I view running as the perfect way of moving. Straight-ahead, rhythmic, unconscious running, that is. I can't see the need to dilute a run with anything foreign."

Another letter came from an East Coast runner. "So you are a rugged long distance runner?" the mimeographed sheet said. "Well, then, an entry is being enclosed to you to enter a real rugged race. The reversible mile!"

The description: "You will be running backwards eight times up and down on the ramp as the race is eight laps. You run the regular way on the straightaway of the course."

That isn't all. Even part of the forward running has a condition attached: "You must extend both your arms at full length sideways and close both your fists, and run in that fashion for 500 paces."

He lists six rules which add up to several steps backwards for running. Each new rule requires an official for enforcement. Each rule makes the runner think about how each step is going down.

At various times I've thought, too, in terms of "ests." Fastest is best. Or longest. Or biggest. Or even weirdest. I've tried to be the fastest miler the state of Iowa ever knew. I've gone out to run 100 miles in a day. I've been responsible, in part, for the massive races around the country. I've helped set up and perpetuate the 24-hour relay, one of the weirdest events ever devised.

I've imagined that running is best at its extremes, and have climbed ladders searching for things I could never find. I've climbed and fallen off a lot of ladders before realizing I was going the wrong way.

Not until I quit struggling upward did I see that the best running is at the base of the ladder — on solid, level ground. Better to keep going in small circles there than to climb higher and higher up a ladder to the inevitable fall from the top.

The sport as a whole is moving up that ladder — in expense, in size, in organization, in eliteness, in weirdness. If that's what you want from it, fine. I'm not telling you to quit playing those games. But what I'm concerned about is the spread of the idea that everyone has to play this way or not at all.

I worry that a generation of runners might get so wrapped up in the frills that they'll miss seeing the substance. I worry that the sport might multiply the very problems it could have cured — the tension, alienation, schlocky mechanical nature of the late 20th century.

Running can be a perfect way to escape the pace, the crush, the controls brought on by too many people trying to do too much too fast. Running, alone and in small groups, at modest distances and moderate speeds, is a cheap, simple, effective antidote to the craziness of modern living. But in large and impersonal crowds which drag a person into efforts he can't handle, running is an extension of the madness.

"We seek individual freedom," wrote Roger Bannister, "in a world that of necessity imposes more and more restrictions. The less we find freedom in our work, the more we shall need to find freedom in the games we play."

I learned long ago that I can't make the world over in my image, not even the runner's world. The best I or anyone can do is stake out a personal "island of sanity." Define its boundaries, decide what and who can roam inside of them, run relaxed and free within this perimeter, and protect it against intruders who would bring in craziness.

I can have all of this without traveling more than 10 miles from home. I don't have to conquer any bigger worlds to be happy in my running.

People who read *Runner's World* might think everything in it is sifted through my prejudices. My own stories obviously are. But many of the others go against my grain and yet are published without editorial comment.

RW lists a new technique or method every issue. Training, diet, tactics, etc. Yet I don't run much differently than I did in the dark ages of 10 years ago. If I'd tried to keep up with all the latest ideas — many of which conflict — they would have driven me nuts a long time ago.

We tell a lot about the biggest races, as if Boston, Charleston, Trail's End, Bay-to-Breakers are the ultimate. Yet it's as rare as a 2:10 marathon when I run a race with more than 50 or 100 people. People become a crowd after that. I like people and hate crowds.

All I want from races is an accurate time from a measured route, and I can have this at a Fun-Run any weekend. All I want from the other days of the week is to run and not be bothered, and I can find a good run wherever there's an open lane.

Anything fancier than these is a bother. And I don't bother with it myself. I only let the frills take up so much space in the magazine because I think this is what readers want. But now I wonder?

English runner Rick Morris wrote this week, "One thing I really don't like about Runner's World is the amount of formulas and graphs you reproduce — the mind-boggling scientific data which tries to reduce people to machines, which given a certain work load will produce specific results.

185

"I realize that a lot of people go to a lot of trouble, time and expense to produce all this complex data. I also realize this is one of the reasons running has advanced so rapidly in the last 20 years. But my advice to the average runner is 'go out and enjoy your running.'"

My sentiments precisely. Forget the formulas. Trust your instincts. Do what feels right. And if it doesn't feel right, do something different.

Be your own star. Be your own hero. Don't let anyone else get your kicks for you.

I've come around over the years to being more impressed by quiet little acts played out in obscurity than by big, splashy productions. For instance, I've written in the magazine several times that I'd rather see 10,000 people each running a mile in seven minutes than one doing a mile in 3:45. I'd prefer to see the grandstands empty and the tracks full rather than the other way around. If those 10,000 people are racers, I'd want them spread out among 100 different races instead of jammed into one spectacular human wave.

It's nice that Frank Shorter won the Olympic Marathon. But I'm far more impressed that 5000 or more Americans no one ever heard of are now running in 150 marathon races across the country. The number of U.S. runners and races has gone up on the order of 10 times in the last 10 years. That means more, to my way of thinking, than a barrel full of Olympic gold medals.

Vladimir Kuts died, of a heart attack, at age 48. Kuts, the double Olympic champion from the Soviet Union, had been one of the moving forces in my early running. I was just starting to notice runners when he won at Melbourne.

After that, Kuts did what all good runners from the '50s did when they were done winning. He retired. Quit running completely. Kuts was always heavy for a distance man. And as soon as he quit burning up thousands of calories a day, his weight ran away from him. He puffed up from a short, muscular 150 pounds to almost 250. The ulcers he'd had as a runner worsened without an outlet for his hard-driving energy. And he developed the heart condition which would kill him far too early.

The world records Vladimir Kuts had set were all blown away within a few years. His two gold medals sat as a taunting reminder of what he had once done. The gold and the records were as worthless as last year's calendar when Kuts tried to fight off the decay of time, tension and the extra 100 pounds he was carrying. He forgot that one only buys health penny by penny, day by day.

The cost is quite small if you put in a little bit every day. But it adds up over the years. On the other hand, debts mount the same way, little by little, until you're as far in the red as Kuts was and you can't buy your way out.

The body is always asking, "Sure, you did something once, but what have you done for me lately?" The good effects of running are perishable. They don't store for very long, so you have to renew them several times a week.

For that reason, people who keep doing a little running are better off than those who did a lot one time or plan to do some sometime, but are doing nothing now. Memories and dreams add nothing to the reservoir of fitness.

The challenge in running, then, is not to aim at doing the things no one else has done, but to keep doing things anyone could do — but most never will.

It's harder sometimes to keep going back over the same ground you've covered a thousand times before than to go someplace you've never been. It's harder to get down to the little, everyday tasks than to get up for the big, special ones.

I'm proudest of the little things I've done in running — the things everyone could do if they would. I haven't done much. I've never, for instance, reached 100 miles in a week. My peak is 85, and I usually run barely half that much. I once ran my miles well under five minutes, but I've never come close to four. Now I'll probably never see the fast side of five again. I've run the marathon 26 times, more often over three hours than under.

Hundreds of people run a hundred or more miles each week. Thousands routinely go under five minutes for the mile and under three hours for the marathon. In these comparisons, I'm nowhere.

But I keep going. In the last 10 years, I've run all but about 30 days. And all but a few of those misses were when I was wearing a cast to the knee. Subtract that time and I've averaged less than one day off per year over the last decade.

Anyone could do that. It amounts to no more than an easy half-hour to hour on most days. That isn't much on a single day, but it adds up to a great deal over a year or 10 or 20 years.

Only rarely do I look that far ahead or behind. I'm having too much fun today to think about a future that may never come and a past that can never live again.

Only by running today can I renew what happened yesterday and build a base for tomorrow. In the end, then, the most important and rewarding run is the small, simple, seemingly insignificant one that started at home in darkness this morning, took me only a couple of miles away to a deserted park and brought me home again at dawn.

20. Lasting

Living a long time involves more than having the right set of parents and staying clear of accidents. Those are matters of chance. There are matters of choice, too — ways of juggling one's lifestyle to promote longevity.

Dr. Alexander Leaf, professor at the Harvard Medical School, has hunted out the world's longest-living populations and tried to figure out why they are so durable. He looked at groups, not individual exceptions to a society's norms.

To find these groups, Dr. Leaf traveled to three remote areas — the Hunza region in Pakistan, Vilcabamba in Ecuador and Abkhazia in the USSR—where men and women routinely see their 100th birthdays and are alive enough to enjoy them.

Leaf wrote in *National Geographic* that the three widely separated groups have several things in common.

1. They live in the mountains, usually at high elevations.

2. The mountainous terrain has cut them off somewhat from the mainstream of modern life.

3. They give high status to the aged, who retain a full role in the community.

4. They eat lightly, and the diets include little or no meat.

5. Their everyday living demands almost constant endurance activity.

189

The physical capacities of these groups most impressed Dr. Leaf. He writes, "The old people of all three cultures share a great deal of physical activity. The traditional farming and household practices demand heavy work, and male and female are involved from early childhood to terminal days.

"Superimposed on the usual labor involved in farming is the mountainous terrain. Simply traversing the hills on foot during the day's activities sustains a high degree of cardiovascular fitness as well as general muscular tone."

Shamed by not being able to keep up with a 106-year-old on a six-hour mountainous hike, the doctor began running when he returned to the United States. He wasn't a mountain farmer, and figured this was the next best exercise for him at age 52.

Even before Dr. Leaf's article in *National Geographic*, much had been written about the people of Hunza. As much of it is fiction as fact, perhaps, but enough is known about the Hunzakuts to say that they are among the fittest residents of this planet.

The kingdom of Hunza, almost two miles high in the Himalayas, has no jails because there is no crime, no hospitals because there is no sickness, no banks because all trading is done by barter among neighbors. Men and women work the fields until well past the age of 100.

This is a land of walkers and runners. Anyone from here can cross on foot the single high mountain pass that connects Hunza with the nearest modern settlement, 60 miles away. Over and back is a day's journey.

Officially, Hunza belongs to Pakistan. But the ties are loose. The land of Hunza is self-contained both physically and emotionally. The people have a separate Hunzakut way

190

of life. Unlike their ever-bickering neighbors on the other side of the mountains, the Hunzakuts haven't been at war in 150 years. Life expectancy in India and Pakistan is among the shortest in the world. In Hunza, men claim to father children after 100.

"We are the happiest people in the world," the Mir (King) of Hunza told Renee Taylor for the book *Hunza Health Secrets*. "We have just enough of everything but not enough to make anyone else want to take it away. You might call this 'the happy land of just enough.'" Hunza is a land that has enough of what it needs because the people don't ask for much, and because no one else wants it badly enough to fight for it.

The people there live long, happy, productive lives partly because they don't concern themselves much with time and age. This frees them from the hurry and worry that comes with alternately trying to rush time and hold it back — both most fruitless and frustrating exercises. The people of Hunza have a grace that comes from flowing with time rather than trying to control it.

Renee Taylor writes, "Time is not measured by clocks or calendars (in Hunza). Time is judged by the changing of the seasons, and each season brings the feeling of newness, not a fear that time is slipping irrevocably away.

"In the West, on the other hand, where lives are dominated by clocks and calendars, we tend to view each passing moment as a little piece of life which has cruelly slipped away from us, never to return. Each such slipping bit of time brings us closer to old age and ultimately to death. We worry so much about growing old that we actually increase the process."

In Hunza, a person's life divides into three periods, the Mir says: "The young years, the middle years, and the rich

191

years. In the young years, there is pleasure and excitement and the yearning for knowledge. In the middle years, there is the development of poise and appreciation, along with the pleasures, the excitement and the yearnings of the young years. In the rich years — by far the best period of all — there is mellowness, understanding, the ability to judge and the great gift of tolerance — all of this combined with the qualities of the two previous periods.

"The keynote of life is growth, not aging. Life does not grow old. The life that flows through us at 80 is the same that energized us in infancy. It does not get old or weak. So-called age is the deterioration of enthusiasm, faith to live and the will to progress."

The Mir adds, "Here, there is time to think only of the necessary things. To worry over such an intangible thing as the ticking of a clock or the turning of a page on a calendar, this is foolishness."

There is no such thing as retirement in Hunza. A Hunzakut works all his life, because if he doesn't he doesn't eat. But far from being necessary drudgery, it is a joy for the Hunzakut to work. Nearly all of them are farmers. They spend long days scraping small amounts of food from the rocky slopes. They're up before dawn and don't come home from the fields until the sun is setting, stopping only twice during the day.

The people of Hunza can work this way — often for a hundred years straight — because of the way they look at and pace their work. Renee Taylor says, "Perhaps aside from the magnificent nutrition of the Hunzakuts (mainly coarse, stone-ground wheat flour and apricots), their mental attitude (is) the key to their extraordinary longevity."

192

They believe that without work, a person is as good as dead. "From the day a Hunzakut is born," the Mir says, "he is never coddled. He keeps active until the day he dies... The idleness of retirement is a much greater enemy to life than work. Our people continue to work by choice."

Renee Taylor observes that "the ability to relax is at the bottom of everything. Watch the Hunza people at work or at rest. They are completely relaxed, completely at ease." This is because they don't fight their work. They enjoy it.

The Mir explains, "Cheerfulness is the best mental tonic. If you enjoy your work, you will do it in a relaxed manner, while hate and grumbling will create tension and the nerves will become jumpy.

"Here in Hunza, each task is done with love. A man is lucky to have a field to work. He is lucky to be able to feel the warm sun and know that his muscles move in rhythm with his work. He is lucky to be able to see the beauty which lies all around him."

All Hunzakuts are endurance athletes who practice all day. They have to work the fields and move long distances on foot. Otherwise, they have no food and no contact with the outside world.

Every other day, a runner travels over the high mountain pass from Hunza to Gilgit. He picks up the mail and runs back. The round trip is about 120 miles. Other Hunzakuts frequently walk the distance, preferring walking to riding a horse.

The Hunza people have dug such a well of endurance that they have plenty of energy left for playing after they're through working. Renee Taylor watched a volleyball game while in Hunza. It matched the young men of the valley against older ones. The youngsters were ages 15-50. The veterans were all over 70. One man was 125.

Taylor writes, "Both teams played a strenuous game in the scorching heat of the afternoon sun. If any player was fatigued at any time during the game, it was not discernible. They all seemed as relaxed and comfortable as though they were playing a friendly game of canasta."

The younger men won, but only by a couple of points. It could have gone either way, and age was not the deciding factor. The writer was amazed at the ability of the older men, and said so to the Mir.

The Mir replied, "When will you people learn that our men of 100 feel no more fatigued than our men of 20? Be careful what you say, or soon you will have our people of over 100 feeling three times their age. And then they will think they are growing old."

Age is not a death warrant. It's an opportunity to grow, to keep moving, to keep enjoying nature and people.

Shirali Mislimov was the world's oldest man when he died at 168. The Soviet citizen had said, "There are two sources of long life. One is a gift of nature, and it is the pure air and clean water of the mountains, the fruit of the earth, peace, rest, the soft and warm climate of the highlands.

"The second source is people. He lives long who enjoys life and who bears no jealousy of others, whose heart harbors no malice or anger, who sings a lot and cries a little, who rises and retires with the sun, who likes to work and knows how to rest."

Larry Lewis of San Francisco ran and worked until a few months before his death at 106. He always hated the word "old."

194

"Never say a person is so many years *old*," Lewis once snapped at a reporter. "Old means dilapidated and something you eventually get rid of, like an old automobile or refrigerator. You're like a violin, a portrait, a wine. You mellow, but you never grow old.

41842990R00110

Made in the USA
Middletown, DE
29 March 2017